I0170792

NOLLYWOOD ON THE PULPIT:
PERFORMANCE IN PENTECOSTALISM

S. PEACE

Published by LibraryX in the United Kingdom

First edition

May 2020

© Sarah Peace

Published under a Creative Commons Attribution-
NonCommercial-NoDerivs License (BY-NC-ND)
The author's permission is required in all other
instances.

The copyright for photographs and illustrations
remains with their respective owners.

A catalogue record for this book is available
from the British Library.

ISBN: 978-0-9931-7514-5

CONTENTS

My interest in Nollywood and Pentecostalism stemmed from growing up in the church and observing with amusement how the performative tropes once relegated to high drama television increasingly made their way to the pulpit.

In recent times, 'new era' Nollywood releases have done away with low-budget aesthetics in favour of sleek productions, comfortably holding their own on Netflix. But new Nollywood, for all its successes, can be said to have alienated early audiences who, if they wished to watch mind-bending sci-fi or thrillers, might simply skip African productions altogether, opting for swashbuckling blockbusters. Nollywood's charm laid precisely in its quirks: the DIY special effects, high pitched confrontations, narrative lyric soundtracks, nonsensical but relatable storylines and the assured comeuppance awaiting evildoers that guaranteed a satisfactory ending followed by the closing supplication; "To God be the glory." Nigerians enjoyed Nollywood in part because the films fulfilled the 'so bad, it's good' criteria. For what might seem like exaggerated performances are merely unfettered extensions of performative tendencies in the way Nigerians speak and act in life. The native tongue frequently calls for emphatic diction to give meaning and amplify intention. In public, women are often pressurised to convey emotion theatrically to dismiss assumptions of guilt, be it the wailing widow expected to mourn perpetually, or the maid obliged to fend off witchcraft accusations. Those occupying junior positions habitually perform acts of respect through curtseying regardless of sincerity. Gesticulation accompanies even the most mundane utterances with men also adopting these conducts. Even heterosexual Nigerian men are not averse to eye-rolling, teeth kissing or finger-snapping, and these quirks were central to the appeal of old Nollywood.

Recent productions have become increasingly polished, written to tackle social and political issues with some targeted at the international festival circuit. However, home audiences have not changed, and they are still seeking spectacle, performances, and manifestations of live happenings that are authentically Nigerian, in the way Nollywood used to be.

Leaders of megachurches meanwhile have filled the void by finessing techniques that borrow from magic, mentalism, and the shock factor of live art to orchestrate miracle performances staged to appear like spontaneous happenings. A number of Nollywood stars that dominated the screens in the 2000s have been ordained to the pulpit, with their sermons offering the ultimate nostalgic experience unparalleled elsewhere.

By doing away with the conventions that defined it to find cosmopolitan audiences further afield, those left behind by Nollywood are compensating for this loss through church attendance. This shift does not necessarily signify fundamentalism but rather, the longing for a platform for expression. Chapter one explores the interwoven relationship and parallels between Nollywood and the Pentecostal movement. Both industries represent key cultural exports and observers recognise the performative tropes formerly relegated to old school Nollywood now prevalent on the Pentecostal stage albeit via YouTube, where a flurry of vaudeville acts grace the pulpit in live stream videos demonstrating exorcisms, astonishing miracle healing, and even resurrection feats.

The capacity of Nollywood to both reflect and influence spiritualist and occult practices is examined in Chapter two, in the case of prophet Eddy Nawgu who met a gory end at the hands of the Bakassi Boys, a notorious vigilante group. But before Nawgu, as revealed in Chapter three, Nigeria had been home to an array of messianic figures who helped to propel the rise of prophetic Pentecostalism. Originating in Ijebu, a place central to the story of Nigerian Pentecostalism which also serves as the birthplace of the *Aladura* movement, it was home to Nigeria's first modern messiah who sought to bring a reign of peace through the amalgamation of Christian and Islamic traditions. Others that followed drew on deep-rooted ancestral beliefs within Yoruba culture to make a case for their preordained descent into the world. By drawing on the mystic aspects of different religious traditions, combined with pressing socio-economic decline, growing wealth disparity, anti-big government sentiments, and most importantly, the need for protection in the ever-raging battle against the spirit world, a succession of messiahs such as Jesu Oyingbo, Jesus of Ikot-Ekpene, Olumba Olumba Obu, Satguru Maharaj Ji and Lady Malaika quickly garnered large cults of followers. Their audacious antics opened the floodgates for a new era of fundamentalism that marks Nigerian Pentecostalism as a phenomenon that is inherently native despite its resonance with other movements elsewhere in the world.

Chapter four explores performativity within miracle performance, not only on the part of preachers but the tendency among audiences to prove themselves as vessels of divinity. For the participant, their rationale can be read either as performative visualisation in anticipation of the miracle or the temporary suspension of rational thought clouded by the desire to experience the supernatural – not unlike those who take pleasure in being tricked by a magician. As competition intensified among Pentecostal leaders, accusations of staged miracles circulated rapidly with some said to borrow from eminent magician Professor

Peller's playbook. Yet some prophets seemed to operate out of a fundamental conviction that the ability to recreate the miracles of the Bible was simply a matter of faith. One of such was the case of Prophet Daniel Abodunrin who met a grisly end in a literal lion's den while trying to prove God's might.

Chapter five examines the overlapping resonances between Nollywood and Pentecostalism in the latter's use of theatrics as a central aspect of its appeal by examining the wild antics of modern-day prophets such as Odumeje the Lion and Jeremiah Fufeyin. In a country where ninety-six per cent assert religious affinity to either Islam or Christianity, Nigerian cultural production – music, film and literature to a large extent has been revolutionised by religion. Moving away from narratives that locate poverty as the underlining factor for rising fundamentalism, Chapter six examines how the almost-equal make-up of two of the main Abrahamic religions fostered competition as both struggled to assert political dominance. The roots of Muslim influence on Yorùbá music such as *wéré, jùjú, fuji,* and *waka,* is contrasted with the rise of militant Islamists who offer a radical understanding of Islam and deem music, film, and literature as *haram* (forbidden). This chapter reveals how in its crusade against women, Boko Haram's insurgency unwittingly reinvigorated the Hausa tradition of romantic fantasy fiction *Littattafan Soyayya*, as the medium through which women and girls living under subjugation momentarily escape the clutches of their captors.

Chapter seven explores the performativity of prayer, which alongside ecstatic praise worship, as well as song and dance to instigate miracles, are rites and bodily expressions that characterise Pentecostalism. Fervent prayer, often manifested through speaking in tongues is considered in broader performative contexts such as lilting, beatboxing, vocal improv and scatting in jazz. This chapter makes the case for how these actions can be reimagined in broader performative contexts and can function beyond worship, serving as an end in themselves by expanding their reach to contemporary audiences who do not seek redemption or experience of the divine. The reimagining of Pentecostalism in its explosive charismatic form can be said to offer minority adherents – women and gay churchgoers a platform for uninhibited expression that is otherwise repressed in much of Nigerian society.

Chapter eight highlights the presence of women worshippers and gay choir members as central to the success of the Pentecostal church in recruiting new members. A paradox is revealed in which the church nurtures, exploits and consumes the creative talents of its queer members yet seemingly denies their sexuality. Through the works of male British-Nigerian artists Rotimi Fani-Kayode, Yinka Shonibare and Iké Udé, Chapter nine examines the black body in performance in relation to spirituality, sexuality, desire, and provocation, through gestures that challenge imposition. Faith as a subject in contemporary art is often a perilous undertaking, yet artists such as John Latham, Andres Serrano, Peter de Cupere and others venture in albeit with much trepidation or, in some cases, numbed by self-censorship on matters relating to Islam. As exemplified in Kanye West's *Sunday Service,* this chapter reimagines the performance of Pentecostal rites in an exhibition context for Instagram-driven audiences for whom spiritual experiences are largely marked by public affirmation. The overall decline in religiosity in the West has positioned galleries and museums as sites of transcendence, creating the possibility that Pentecostal performance removed from its natural habitat can still possess the capacity to offer an ethereal experience.

In the same way that Nollywood thrived on establishing a localised voice that was reflective of audiences, Nigerian Pentecostals have reimagined the fellowship of Christ in ways that echo deep-rooted traditional practices. Chapter ten looks at the boom in global Pentecostalism and its expansion from Africa to the West, a return to source termed the 'reverse mission.' By homing in on challenges that markedly affect migrant communities, Pentecostal leaders in capital cities such as London are shifting tack from prosperity teachings to the social gospel, encouraging renunciation of gang membership among black male youths. But the church's desire to intervene amidst governmental cuts to social provisions in a bid to acquire younger audiences comes with a price – the demand for accountability at a scale previously unheard of in its home setting, where abuse and exploitation have often gone unchecked.

CHAPTER 1

Nollywood and Pentecostalism

Nigerian cinema colloquially known as Nollywood, has a history that dates back over one hundred years. Disregarding foreign productions in the colonial era, early releases largely strived to archive the indigenous travelling theatre tradition on film. Those concerns soon made way for direct-to-video films with the increasing proliferation of digital technology amplified by the unprecedented success of Kenneth Nnebue's *Living in Bondage* (1992). The sector experienced a boom in the mid-2000s quickly earning a reputation for being the second-largest film industry in the world only behind Bollywood. With an output of more than two thousand films a year, it churns out more feature films than Hollywood and is commercially the third highest-ranking producer in the world. With an audience of approximately fifteen million people per release, its most popular outputs maintained the winning formula of exaggerated performances, overwritten scripts, impassioned high-pitched dialogue and relatable subject matters with a recurrent theme of good versus evil. Formerly perceived as low brow due to its reliance on low-budget VFX and simplistic storylines, some considered the films denigrating, as they were thought to encapsulate the worst of Nigerian culture. In recent years, the 'new wave' era has seen productions tackle meatier plotlines with glossy finishes and few films now leave the editing suite without the obligatory drone and tracking shots. Haynes (2016) cites Kunle Afolayan's 2009 feature *The Figurine: Araromire* as the pivotal production that kickstarted the new era. The industry can today boast of an Oscar-nominated release although the accolade for Genevieve Nnaji's directorial debut *Lionheart* (2018) was short-lived.

Nollywood, like Nigeria's music and fashion industries, relies on establishing particular tropes and conventions which are almost uniformly followed across the board, enabling consumers to gain quick familiarisation with the latest offerings.

The permeance of Nollywood in everyday life in Nigeria is ubiquitous, looming large in the public consciousness. Actors routinely command larger followings than politicians, who themselves are known for their excesses. A common truth is the rags-to-riches story of each famous face, finding success in an industry that unlike its Indian counterpart, few hail from acting dynasties. Newcomers can hold a reasonable expectation of meritocracy and few superstars would admit to being an *ajebutter* (someone born with a silver spoon). In a country where notions of beauty are vast and much more expansive than in the West, performers are afforded the freedom of appearing as their authentic selves, even if, and especially when that veracity comes across as *razz*, a way of being and form of raw expression that does away with all pretence, embracing native vernacular, regional dialects, or rural mannerisms demonstrated in the success of content producers such as Mark Angel. Anything goes; tribal marks, birthmarks, one can be fat, short, lanky, *lepa*, be a dwarf, be an *oyinbo pepper*, be black like Baba Sala, be mixed-race, be an albino, or have a visible disability – talent is simply recognised on merit. This combined with the strong Nigerian belief in destiny - the idea that outcomes are only determined by the will of the gods or God informs how the notion of fame is perceived. As is explored in subsequent chapters, this principle also underlines the belief that people become eligible for blessings at designated times, expressed by the willingness of ordinary people to take the stage to perform miracles. Having dethroned Genevieve Nnaji to the 'Queen of Nollywood' title, Omotola Jalade enjoys a career kickstarted by one such encounter. A graduate of Estate Management with no formal training in acting, Jalade had accompanied a friend to an audition where the spotlight was unexpectedly thrown onto her and two decades later, she has appeared in more than 300 films and is now a voting member on the Oscars' Academy board. Therefore, the idea that anybody can be a star if they possess talent and it is their 'time to shine', is a resonant credence among the populace.

Breaking away from other Methodist factions, new Pentecostals have relegated theology and teaching of the doctrine to a secondary role, bringing worship to centre stage through performance. Emphasis is placed on creating visual spectacles reminiscent of Nollywood flicks. If one of the tenets of Christianity is for followers save as many lives as possible by bringing them to Christ, Pentecostals carry out that obligation by showing rather than telling the benefits of salvation. Due to its sheer scale and sometimes unconventional spatial aesthetics, some observers have contextualised the Pentecostal megachurch as a 'non-place' but rather than this understanding that posits it as a transient site, perhaps the megachurch has created a new category that expands how churches are conceived in the modern age. Sanders (2014) draws comparisons between megachurches and shopping centres as transitory sites that often lack any distinguishing historical, cultural or geographical anchor points, leaving visitors with a sense of being nowhere in particular. Indeed, Pentecostal churches are known to take over nondescript sites such as car parks, campus grounds, cinemas, theatres, and warehouses for festivals and conventions. Sanders aptly identifies how the megachurch is being consumed by the banality of global capitalism with overarching emphasis placed on entertainment, showmanship and the transactional dynamic between the house and its guests. However, this view overlooks the fact that Nigerians themselves are the fiercest critics of the booming Pentecostal movement, though many steadfastly cling to their church tribe as the true believers.

For many Pentecostals, activities such as tobacco and alcohol consumption, recreational drug use, clubbing and premarital sex while not explicitly forbidden, are typically not routine. For them, the Sunday service gathering replaces bars and nightclubs as the avenue in which socialising and entertainment takes place. The innate human desire to participate in collective activities such as dancing, music appreciation, striking friendships, expanding professional networks, making local connections, playing voyeur and for some, taking pride in being seen presumably at their best, are all fulfilled through church attendance. Sociological studies have shown that there are various benefits to be found in participating in group worship and collective dance such as increased self-confidence.

Ironically, the church becomes a site in which women can experience momentary bouts of freedom unafforded elsewhere. In many urban contexts, Nigerian women might experience aggression or assault from *area boys* if their dress code is deemed sexually suggestive and typically, the woman would be blamed in such a scenario. On the streets, men determine the codes of conduct – yet within the confines of the church, those power dynamics are suspended. A young woman can in the context of frenzied spirit worship, remove layers of clothing and writhe around on the stage as the Holy Spirit consumes her body. The same onlookers who would scorn such bodily expressions in public would relate to it as a divine intercession when performed at the pulpit.

It is no coincidence that film set designers are drafted in to build church podiums complete with red carpets that flow from the aisles over the stage steps, spilling onto the podium. On the pulpit, grand arrangements of flowers, ornate tapestry and gold trimmings are used to evoke celestial settings. Traditional symbols such as the cross, stained glass, organs, wooden pews, and vaulted ceilings are replaced with HD screens, hi-tech sound systems, laser beams, fog machines, with seating arrangements and lighting not unlike that of concert venues. With cameras beaming the action on television and live stream, the tendency for individuals within the audience to exhibit performative displays are almost on par with that of the preachers orchestrating the show.

On Nollywood's silver screen, audiences are accustomed to sleepy scenes playing out in excruciating detail on the banal, edited to encourage dialogue between viewers – yet the script makes sudden leaps to highly consequential actions. But the frenetic change in pace which might throw non-native audiences is a welcome shift for its primary market, who understand fully well that a Nollywood experience is incomplete if solitary. Films are not watched passively; viewers actively engage with the screen and each other with physical responses ranging from laugh out loud moments, disgusted hisses, finger snapping, astonished slow clapping and foot-stomping with running commentaries throughout, especially in settings such as the beauty salon.

With old Nollywood budgets averaging ₦2 million (£4,000) per release, producers perform little short of a miracle to realise each project. Unlike their western counterparts, amateur filmmakers in Nigeria earn a living from their craft and often wrap up feature-length productions in as little as two weeks. The sector generates revenues of $600 million annually and employs more than one million people. Single-take setups and confrontations staged outdoors rather than within interior spaces are commonplace. The frequent use of natural light in outdoor settings means NEPA's erratic electricity supply does not massively disrupt tight production schedules.

On the screen, characters function in starkly real settings where little window dressing is added - from lavish marble-floored echoey mansions to *face-me-I-face-you* lodgings complete with surplus bodies on the street, just standing, gawking, and waiting. These bodies are the real-life crowd that seemingly appear out of thin air as soon as anything happens in public. They are the people who intervene as you haggle with the *Okada* man for your change, or help you push your car after a breakdown or give you unsolicited guidance as you park – especially if you are a woman. Just as they emerge from nowhere in real life, they appear in the corners of the screen and filmmakers do not bother removing them, for they are a fabric of the scene. Some might call them 'Lagos lookers', but they can also be referred to in Yorùbá as *awon aiye* (the people of the world). Thus, Nigerians can seldom watch Nollywood and fail to see representations of themselves.

Beyond Nigerian cinema, the tendency for public performative expression is deep-rooted within Yoruba tradition in rituals such as *Egúngún* ceremonies. The Yoruba possess a long history of dance, music, theatre, and folklore tradition imbibed within their cultural landscape. Storytelling dramatised through theatre and performance long stood at the heart of community rituals with plays used to preserve ancestral and cultural history, express discontent against the ruling classes and serve as a means of imparting moral values. The various types of masquerade dance, rituals and rites dating back to the 14th century which are rooted in ancestor reverence and spirit worship all come to the fore in the reimagining of African Pentecostalism.

As one of the largest cultural exports of Nigeria, Nollywood provided a blueprint for contemporary Pentecostal leaders to establish a subcategory of Christianity that rests on the primary tenet of showmanship though miracle performance. In Nigeria's rapidly growing image economy in which entertainment increasingly converges with religion, Nollywood stars of yesteryear are finding new platforms on the pulpit. Screen legends Liz Benson, Eucharia Anunobi, Hilda Dokubo and Patience Ozokwor along with their male counterparts Zack Orji, Kanayo O. Kanayo, Charles Okafor, and Larry Koldsweat have all been ordained as reverends and prophets with significant followings to boot.

Akin to the audience immersion in the films, there are overlaps in the bodily responses that the congregation brings to church services. Like their counterparts in Nollywood, they can be seen to 'chew the scenery' as if their melodramatic performance has indeed been written into the script.

CHAPTER 2

Spirit, law, and order

So deeply is spiritualism embedded into the Nigerian psyche that it is practised not only in private life but collectively and publicly. In some cases, it has been government-sanctioned and implemented as a tool for policing. One of such examples is the reign of the Bakassi Boys.

In response to a spate of armed robberies that terrorised residents and businesses in Abia State in the late 1990s, a clique of agile young men comprised mostly of market traders formed a coalition to fight back. The group took their name from the Bakassi province in the South East, the oil-rich peninsula that had long been at the centre of a territorial struggle between Nigeria and Cameroon. The conflict led to the rise of numerous paramilitary groups such as *The Bakassi Movement for Self Determination*, which operated with a bottom-up anarchic regime. Their modus operandi revealed a blueprint that may have served to inspire the Bakassi Boys.

The Abia State invaders had been reported to use black magic to disorient their victims before kidnapping them for money rituals that relied on blood sacrifice. The kidnappings, murders and ritual cannibalism of children were becoming a plague on the region. Those perpetrating the crimes were generally understood to be working for prominent figures among the elites and the new money class who were deemed untouchable. The police were seemingly rendered useless because they were thought to either be in the pay of those responsible or simply unequipped to deal with the matter. As a result, herbalists and medicine men who offered protection became central to survival.

The Bakassi operated with such efficiency that corrupt police, religious leaders and local chiefs began to fear them, as they adopted a strategy that combined physical prowess with occult divination to outwit and snare their prey. The success of their campaigns led them to be officially recognised and funded by the governor, with neighbouring states of Anambra and Imo entrusting their security to them.

Situated around semirural localities of the South East, a culture of deep-rooted traditional spiritual practices thrived enabling them to expand their remit to eliminating witches and sorcerers. Positing themselves as judge, jury and executioner, jungle justice was swiftly served to suspects and the Bakassi strongmen were said to have executed 3,000 alleged wrongdoers within a period of eighteen months.[1] The spate of vigilante killings eventually built up to an incredible climax in the case of a famed spirit man, who proved to be their most prominent casualty - the self-styled prophet of God, Eddy Nawgu.

---

[1] News Service Enugu, February 2002 (From Harnischfeger, J., (2006))

Born Edward Okeke, Nawgu's moniker reflected his heritage from the Nawgu community in the Dunukofia region of Anambra state. In 1986, the then 29-year-old Okeke declared he had been touched by God and bestowed with the ability to intercept the spiritual realm. He established a church called the Anioma Healing Centre and began performing miracles, healing the sick and restoring vision to the blind. Like Jesus of Nazareth, he soon became known as Eddy *na* Nawgu (Eddy from Nawgu) for his prophetic declarations and ability to conjure a change in the fortunes of those who sought his counsel. Ten years later, his client base had expanded to include prominent figures from Nigeria's high society including celebrities, entertainers and politicians. Soon he accumulated an extensive financial portfolio and married a woman who bore him eight children – all supposed symbols of God's favour. In the grounds of his church, a life-size statue depicted him attaining victory over the enemy who had been conquered and beheaded, mimicking Donatello's sculpture of David. In his office hung photographs of his clients which included state governors and ex-presidents. But word on the streets suggested Nawgu's apparent gift of prophecy was, in fact, a manifestation of the demonic arts. By the mid-1990s, rumours began spreading about the practice of human sacrifice in his church. Through 1999 and into 2000, protests at the offices of the then Anambra state governor Dr Chinweoke Mbadinuju intensified over the disappearance of people thought to have been used for Nawgu's blood rituals. At this point, Nawgu was said to be at the helm of a mob-style operation with his own goons that seized people for rituals and human sacrifice. It was claimed that his victims were buried alive on the grounds of the church to ensure his continued success. Newspapers reported that sixteen newborns who disappeared from a maternity unit at a hospital in Onitsha were traced to him. Many similar reports were printed and soon he was said to be liable for a body count of ninety-three missing people.

Despite the media frenzy and public outcry, no one seemed to be following up with action in making arrests or holding him to account. Nawgu occupied such a frightening space in the imagination of the locals that he was commonly believed to be otherworldly, often referred to as the Spirit Man. Among the Igbo, he was called *Alusi N'eje Uka*[2] (The deity who goes to church). As such, locals could only look to the Bakassi for help in conquering the sorcerer.

Following the transition from a military to a civilian government in the country in 1999, people had little confidence in the Nigerian police to manage the rising rate of violent crime due to endemic criminal collusion. With protests intensifying, the Bakassi militia were greenlighted to see to the matter. The Bakassi who until then had not failed to apprehend a suspect would find their greatest challenge in Nawgu. Armed with combatant weapons and *juju* (ritual charms), they launched thirteen operations to capture the prophet, all of which failed. It was reported in the press that Nawgu could not be caught since he possessed the ability to teleport himself across space and time. The Bakassi consulted with senior military advisors and employed some intervention from their supreme spiritual leader, who led the final operation with a series of incantations

---

[2] In the Igbo tradition and religion, *Alusi* are spirits that are worshiped and honoured. In the Igbo spiritual mythology, several realms exist including the realm of the living, the realm of the ancestors, and the realm of the unborn. As divinities, *Alusi* are believed to operate across the realms.

on their arrival at Nawgu's compound. On November 4, 2000, which marked their fourteenth attempt, the Bakassi finally ensnared the Spirit Man. Stripped of his mystic gifts, the captured Nawgu was led out of his home enchained.

During the five days he was detained, a signed confession was extracted from him in which he admitted his guilt over the kidnappings and human sacrifices. High profile politicians and officials including former president Ibrahim Babangida interceded for Nawgu's release from the hands of the merciless Bakassi to no avail. Fragmented clips of Nawgu's interrogation and confession were released to the press to justify their refusal to release him to the police, as the Bakassi made the case for circumventing formal criminal justice proceedings. The prophet's fall from power was sensationalised in the media and a bootleg audio cassette titled *The Original True Confession of Prophet Eddy Nawgu,* rapidly circulated on the streets. Nawgu pleaded to deaf ears that he should be thrown alive into the turbulent River Niger, insisting that water spirits would punish him accordingly. To satisfy the people that the dreaded Nawgu had indeed been slain, his execution was performed at the Ochanja market in Onitsha where a crowd of twenty thousand people gathered to watch him beheaded, after which his body was chopped into pieces and charred to ensure his spirit did not return for vengeance.

The unhinged reign of the Bakassi Boys was depicted in part in Lancelot Imaseun's action flick *Issakaba* (2000) with the title being an anagram for its subject. The release inspired many copycat Nollywood productions based on vigilante justice and money ritual themes. The demise of Nawgu was illustrated in graphic posters serving as both a cautionary tale against abominable acts of false prophesy and as a symbol of vestige celebrating the triumph of the Bakassi Boys. The hand-drawn cartoons depicted Nawgu with a prominent potbelly to emphasise his greed. In one poster Nawgu is labelled an 'imitation prophet' and shown coercing the minds of his congregation. Reducing them to dry bones in his shrine, his magical powers were amplified. Following his capture, he confesses to killing ninety-five virgins and a further massacre of four hundred people. With a hungry crowd baying for his blood, Nawgu is told by the executioner, "you must reap what you sow!" Once the sword slices through his neck, his body is hacked to pieces and scorched, with cautionary texts bleeding off the poster warning; *"THE SINNER SHALL NOT GO UNPUNISHED"*.

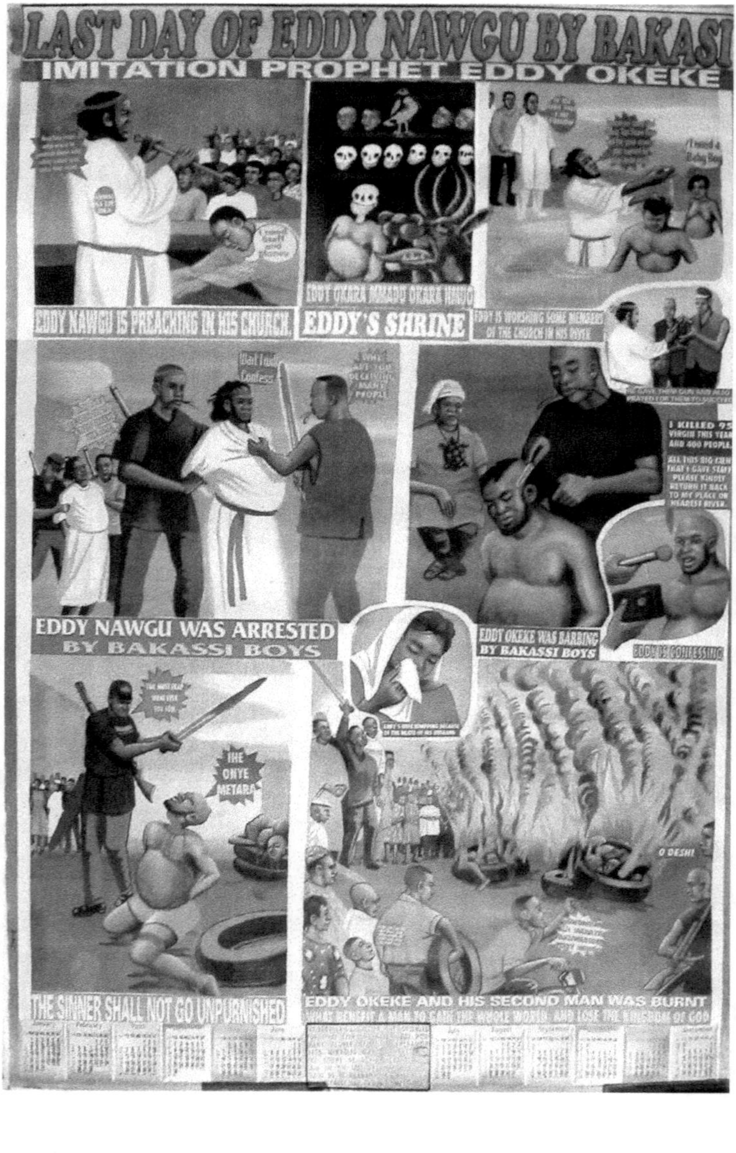
LAST DAY OF EDDY NAWGU BY BAKASI
IMITATION PROPHET EDDY OKEKE
EDDY NAWGU IS PREACHING IN HIS CHURCH.
EDDY'S SHRINE
I KILLED 95
VIRGIN THIS YEAR
AND 400 PEOPLE.
EDDY NAWGU WAS ARRESTED
BY BAKASSI BOYS
EDDY OKEKE WAS BARBING
BY BAKASSI BOYS
EDDY IS CONFESSING
IHE ONYE METARA
O DESHI
THE SINNER SHALL NOT GO UNPURNISHED
EDDY OKEKE AND HIS SECOND MAN WAS BURNT

CHAPTER 3

Magicians and messiahs

Before Nawgu, prophecy and the occult were perceived to be at odds with each other since the former was a gift given to those who were chosen by God and the latter was seen as the Devil's work. Following the rise and fall of Prophet Eddy, a growing cloud of suspicion arose around the leadership of Nigeria's modern megachurches such as the Synagogue Church of All Nations led by TB Joshua, boasting millions of members in its congregation. Despite no other investment portfolios apart from extensions of his ministry, its leader's personal wealth was estimated by Forbes in 2011 to be approximately $10-15 million. In 2016, Joshua was accused of employing black magic to achieve his successes by Bishop Kayode Peller. For years, it had been rumoured that the spiritualist Olumba Olumba bestowed Joshua with the powers of the occult and similar accusations had been thrown around, but Peller's charge raised eyebrows since the accuser was a former magician and the son of the celebrated Nigerian magician Professor Peller.

As a young man, Bishop Peller had followed his father's path into performing magic under the stage name of The Fantastic Young Peller and established his church with a brand name alluding to his sleight of hand proficiency. The aptly named Fingers of God Church in Alagbado which is modest in comparison to Joshua's is not advertised as a site for deliverance, miracles or wonders. It welcomes a small audience of regular members and is one of the few 'Bible-believing' factions among Nigerian Pentecostals who focus on theological scholarship.

Given Joshua's dominance of the Pentecostal circuit, Peller's claim made headlines as he outrightly denounced the absence of any divine presence in Joshua's ministry. Rather he claimed to recognise in Joshua many techniques employed by stage magicians such as hypnosis and mentalism while he performed his 'drama of healing.' He described the relationship between Joshua and his audience as a process of seduction in which the conjurer could influence the susceptible mind of the audience. Having walked away from the world of magic, he now dismissed it as a form of 'demonic power' which for him, stood at odds with Christianity. Peller boldly insisted that the miracles performed by Joshua were achieved by placing his subjects in a state of temporary hypnosis and once they left the four walls of the church, their troubles resumed again. Defending his position, Peller said, "Let nobody think that I am jealous of them (TB Joshua and Chris Oyakhilome) because their churches are big. If I want to make mine big, I know what to do. I am the son of Peller. I know where things happen."[3]

---

[3] Daily Post (February 2016) *T. B. Joshua, Oyakhilome use magic on their followers – Former magician, Bishop Peller* Dailypost.ng

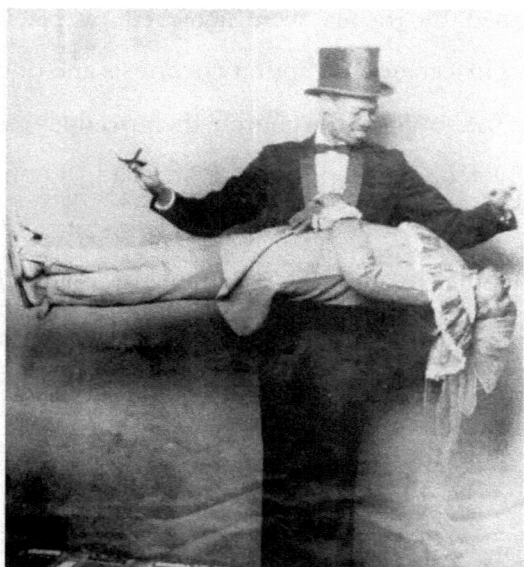

Professor Peller and Lady Peller (Alhaja Silifat Adeboyin) performing in 1969

Professor Peller

Peller's father - born Moshood Folorunsho Abiola emerged on the Nigerian entertainment scene in the 1960s offering a startling change to much of what people of the newly independent nation had ever witnessed. Abiola drew on his training at a school of magic in India where lessons would have included disappearing acts, sword slicing stunts, levitation and money doubling tricks, all of which are tied together with dramatic and comedic delivery. On his return to Nigeria, Abiola began performing in his signature tailcoat suit, bow tie, bowler hat and wand, adopting the quintessential European approach to the showmanship of magic to create the persona of Professor Peller. Magic had long been a fabric of Nigeria's indigenous religions and traditions with rituals often utilised to fulfil individualistic action or to serve a practical function such as wielding weaponry, healing, divination and revealing truths about the past and the future. Thus, magic functioned as a tool rather than an end in itself. Peller's entry onto the scene would completely transform the place of magic within

Nigeria's cultural landscape.

Described by fans as suave and majestic, Peller's set often featured a series of escalating feats from rudimentary hat and dove tricks to sword-swallowing. However, the showstopping routine was the one in which he would slice his wife Lady Peller in two halves with an electric saw and feign panic at not being able to put her back together again. Each time, the audience was led to believe that they were witnessing an illusion gone wrong. As the frenzied audience hollered, the moment of prestige would finally come as his beautiful assistant sprang out from within the crowd. Shocked audience members would scream and flee at the thought of their close encounter with a ghost.[4]

Peller was said to have enthralled even the toughest of Africa's military leaders and the nobility. His patronage included President Gnassingbe Eyadema of Togo, President Samuel Doe of Liberia, the president of the Benin Republic Mathieu Kerekou, Nigeria's

---

[4] It was from my mother that I first heard the story of Professor Peller. Although she insists on her inability to remember events, she never fails to recall in vivid detail the night she encountered Peller at his show at the Obisesan Hall in Ibadan around 1978. Despite the passage of time, she remains in awe at the orchestration of Lady Peller's resurrection feat and contends that Peller was simply lucky to pull off the trick on that occasion.

Chief Obafemi Awolowo, Alhaji Lateef Jakande, as well as his contemporaries in the entertainment industry such as Fela Kuti and veteran Yorùbá film actor and musician Moses Olaiya aka Baba Sala.

As Peller enjoyed a meteoric ascent to fame, envy took hold among other performers on the magic circuit and a fierce rivalry developed with a magician known as Aladokun of Ikirun who dominated the scene until Peller's return from India. Peller's rival was a native of Osun State who practised traditional sorcery and as such, viewed Peller not only as a threat but as disloyal to the tradition. Aladokun performed barefoot, adorned with cowrie shells, bodypainting and garments woven from plants and silkworm, with feats facilitated by incantations, chants and conjuring. He would have used props such as freshly beheaded chickens dripping blood and smoke-filled calabashes. Peller on the other hand, presented himself as a learned modern master, employing the use of sound, design, technology, and specialised equipment to create illusions.

At the height of their rivalry, a wild urban myth originating from Aladokun's camp began circulating about a contest of power in which the two magicians asserted brute strength over the other. The incident was narrated to prove Aladokun's superiority borrowing from the story of the feat of serpents in the Book of Exodus. Just like Aaron's snake swallowed the snakes conjured up by the Pharaoh's magician's, Aladokun astonishingly claimed to have swallowed Peller whole but mercifully spat him out again. Yet, Aladokun found himself left behind, disappearing into obscurity as Nigerians increasingly embraced the emergence of international music, film, art and entertainment from India, China and Europe.

As a devout Muslim, Peller was known to observe the call to prayer five times daily. Alongside Islam, he practised mysticism and had revealed to journalists that the only time he failed to wear the ritual objects he believed protected him was during his prayers. Fate would strike at one such time as Peller was assassinated by gunmen while praying at his home on August 2, 1997 and to this day, his murder has not been solved. Coincidentally, Peller died on the same day as his friend, the legendary Fela Kuti. The news of Kuti's death overshadowed all other events such that Peller's understated exit seemed like another disappearing act and he continued to live on in the minds of many.

Peller's work and influence during his short-lived career would have lasting ramifications on the growing Pentecostal movement in the years that followed, as the explosion of healing ministries coincided with reports of 'fake miracle machines' and other magic apparatus used by preachers. A combination of factors including the decline of state authority, the precarious nature of life, and paltry to non-existent social provisions created crippling conditions that allowed a wave of prophets, messiahs, and miracle workers to flourish, fuelling the rise of the Nigerian Pentecostal movement.

The Ijebu region in the south-west is the setting in which the *Aladura* movement took off, serving as the foundational roots of Nigeria's Pentecostal movement. Clarke (1995) proposes that pre-colonial Ijebuland was also home to the local Mahdiyya movement which birthed Nigeria's first modern self-proclaimed messiah, Muhammad Jumat Imam. Borrowing from tenets of the broader Mahdi belief common across West Africa which holds the promise of a saviour continuing Prophet Muhammad's work, combined with Marxist concepts of utopianism and secular thought, Jumat renounced jihad and the spread of Islam by the sword, seeking to bring a reign of peace. He declared himself the 'Mahdi of the Muslims and the Messiah of the Christians' offering freedom from a world plagued by tyranny.

Of the many prophets that have come and gone, a handful made such an impression in the minds of Nigerians that decades after their reign, their antics are still told to spine-tingling effect. Their presence was significant because it underscores the phenomenon of Nigerian Pentecostalism as a movement that is inherently native.

Jesu Oyingbo

Emmanuel Odumosu also known as *Jesu Oyingbo* (Jesus of *Oyingbo*) born in 1915 was a self-proclaimed messiah and founder of the Universal College of Regeneration. Sometime in the 1950s he declared himself the Second Coming, building his mythology on his heritage as the grandson of a revered traditional healer in Ijebu Ode. Odumosu's philosophy was strongly tied to sexual liberation, uninhibited sexual expression, communal living and self-sufficiency.

Before his reinvention, he had trained as a carpenter and like many men of his generation, he served during World War II while Nigeria was a British colony. After the war, Odumosu was relieved of his duties in the post and telegraph department but struggled to find meaningful work and was imprisoned for six months for defaulting on payments due to creditors. During this period of disillusion, he attended various Protestant churches in Lagos and soon began to experience dreams and visions. For him, the visions were incredibly profound, and he drew parallels between his own life and that of Christ. Although the two men had little in common beyond carpentry, Odumosu believed that he had been chosen as the successive messiah that would redeem the modern world.

In 1952, the charismatic Odumosu began giving public sermons that combined Yorùbá and Christian beliefs, such as the duality of the world as both a physical and spiritual place but drawing on postmodern concepts about discipline and sacrifice laced with empowering messages of self-reliance. He taught his followers how to equip themselves with the necessary tools to navigate a dark reality in which evil spirits were constantly engaged in battle with them in the physical world. In the early days, his followers were prohibited from consuming alcohol or tobacco and engaging in casual sex but that would change over time.

In the mid-1950s, a patron gifted him with a large mass of land in Maryland, Lagos which he deemed the 'New Jerusalem', and he encouraged his followers to move in and pay rent to him rather than to commercial landlords or local government. He expanded his following by regularly preaching and performing miracles at Oyingbo market and as his following grew, he exerted dominance over male converts through initiation rites where they were each lashed nine times with a whip. He also had sexual relations with his followers' wives, sisters and daughters, many of whom fell pregnant with his children. The women were said to have submitted themselves to Odumosu and far from subjugation, they regarded their cooperation as a religious obligation to the sect (Ojo, 2005). According to Odumosu's daughter Adeyinka, he fathered 153 children with forty-six women[5] and had over 2,000 followers residing in his spiritual enclave. The commune featured prominent statues of Christian and traditional pagan figures and the grounds included a hospital, salon, cinema, library, printing press, a primary and secondary school as well as a bakery famed locally for its delicious 'good luck' bread. The secret ingredients used in the addictive bread would later develop its own myths that still linger today. Since Odumosu's project existed as a self-sustained economy, the occurrences went unreported in their time. Details about the sect largely came to light only when an international legal brawl ensued among his wives and children following his death.[6]

Odumosu died aged 72 on January 17, 1988. Unlike Jesus of Nazareth, *Jesu Oyingbo* failed to (be seen to) resurrect on the third day as he had promised. Nonetheless, Odumosu should be credited with kickstarting the cult of the prophet in Nigeria.

---

[5] Punch Newspapers (2018) *Dad never collected tithe, offering from his congregation — Jesu Oyingbo's daughter*. Punchng.com

[6] The New York Times. Onishi, N. (1998) *Lagos Journal; After Carnival of 'Second Coming,' an Apocalypse*. Nytimes.com

Jesus of Ikot-Ekpene

Also born in 1915 was a man who came to be known as Jesus of Ikot-Ekpene. Although a contemporary of Jesu Oyingbo with actions that mirrored one another's, there is no record of them ever meeting and each remained rooted within the community they served, where they lived and died. Both practised mentalism and wielded power over thousands of people, creating empires built on professing to be the Saviour.

Etim 'Edidem' Bassey was born in the state of Akwa Ibom in the city of Ikot-Ekpene, a place of historic and religious significance under British rule. Located near the southern coast, the city was one of the first destinations for British missionaries who tasked themselves with converting the populace from animism to Christianity. Since the native people practised their religion as part of everyday life, Christian rituals were merely adapted into existing traditions failing to replace it entirely as witnessed in some other parts of Nigeria. Reminiscent of the Rastafarian movement in Jamaica fusing Hebrew and

Christian practices with Afro-Caribbean culture, or the hybrid religion created by Latin American natives combining Catholicism with Voodoo and Santería practices, the people of the 'south-south' of Nigeria created a cultural-religious fusion that welcomed an ever-changing array of religious practices. It was under this climate of cultural syncretism and appropriation which continued to mutate over time, that Jesus of Ikot-Ekpene emerged.

No records exist of Bassey's education at the local missionary schools, but he regularly attended English-taught Sunday school at the local Methodist church. It was later claimed that his knowledge of English and other languages were divinely imparted. The myth-building around Jesus of Ikot-Ekpene began in 1935 when a conflict arose in the church between the European evangelists and the African priests-in-training. Bassey intervened and announced he would withdraw into the wilderness to pray until peace reigned. It was said that his prayers were so effective in mediating matters that some church members volunteered to join him in the forest. As the fasting and prayers intensified and dragged on for weeks, they witnessed his delirious decline and soon left one after another. It was during this period of isolation that he claimed to have had an encounter with the Son of God.

Bassey revealed that Christ appeared to him and told him that he had been chosen to be the 'king of the Gentiles.' Afterwards, he claimed he was suddenly able to speak English, German and French fluently, supposedly evidence of his divine encounter. But the coastal cities in the south of Nigeria have historically drawn bilingual migrants, refugees and settlers from neighbouring countries including French and German-speaking Cameroon, Benin, and Togo. Nonetheless, Bassey's origin story was being constructed as he began to publish and disseminate literature, taking to public squares to perform miracles which included the resurrection of a boy who had died in his mother's arms. He returned to his hometown of Ikot-Ekpene and established the Spiritual Kingdom Church of Christ (SKCC) naming the building *The Throne of God*.

For his followers, any unusual occurrences in the church were considered to be signs that their leader was indeed the Chosen One. During the supernatural encounter in which he claimed Christ had ordained him a king, he had been presented with a vision of himself positioned on a golden throne. He ordered his followers to build the throne but on completion, he announced that it should be stored away in the church vestry. During this time, the building was infested by termites that destroyed the wooden pews and every other furniture – all except the throne, which would have been sealed with gold varnish. For his followers, the miracle of the untarnished throne was further evidence of Bassey's anointing and they began to call him *Edidem*, the *Efik* word for king.

Like Jesu Oyingbo, Edidem too had grown up without a father figure in his life and as a young man had struggled to keep a failing business afloat. He however possessed a charismatic persona and was well-versed in the art of persuasion. He too imparted his masculine dominance over his female followers irrespective of their marital status. His mere mortal followers considered it a privilege to be chosen to fulfil his sexual needs since an encounter with 'the king' was akin to sleeping with God himself. He married twelve of his female followers and appointed them his disciples.

Through his ministry, Edidem accumulated an enormous portfolio of wealth and the Nigerian press acknowledged him as the richest man in Akwa Ibom. From existing photographs, Edidem's appearance seemed grandiose and otherworldly, reminiscent of an Arabian prince from a time long gone. Often draped in Middle Eastern silk tunics fastened with ranked belts, he adorned his head with either a diamond and ruby-encrusted crown or an ornate *agal* traditionally made from goat fur woven with gold thread. His neck, wrists and fingers dazzled in gold trinkets with his eyes peering out from behind black sunglasses. Always seen in his right hand, a golden sceptre.

In an annual event, Edidem would sit on his golden throne, not unlike the Pope's traditional *sedia gestatoria* and be paraded through the city to jubilant crowds hoping to be blessed by the sight of his holiness. To this day, he is celebrated by his followers at the start of each year with a procession and his resting place is venerated as a shrine. Successive generations of leaders in his sect are assigned the role of 'Custodian Lords of the Throne.' In honour of the 'holy king', his followers and spiritual children add the moniker 'Edidem' to their names and it represents the most popular surname in the region. Today, the city of Ikot-Ekpene per square mile has one of the highest concentrations of churches in the world.

Olumba Olumba Obu

Assigned the patronymic name of Olumba Olumba, Obu was born in Cross Rivers State on December 31, 1918. Aged 38, he established the Brotherhood of the Cross and Star (BCS), a sect that was the first of its kind in Nigeria. Olumba's teachings played on the aspect of the Holy Spirit within the Christian doctrine of the Trinity and spirit presence in Yorùbá religion to launch his own brand of spiritualism. For many Africans, the question of the spirit was never about debating the existence of the supernatural, but decoding spiritual forces as either good or evil and Olumba's intervention addressed this squarely.

Unlike Jesu Oyingbo and Jesus of Ikot-Ekpene, Olumba was widely believed to be a spiritualist of the Satanist variety evidenced by the demotion of Jesus in the sect, and Olumba's penchant for appearing head to toe in red. The image he cultivated around BCS was that of a shrine rather than a church and its branches are referred to as bethels. Adherents believed Olumba was literally a physical manifestation of God and considered Christ to be a lesser prophet, and that he had been sent into the world to complete the unfinished task of saving mankind. Within the sect, prayers are performed in reverence to photographs of Olumba. He claimed to have performed his first miracle just days after his birth. His arrival in the region of Biakpan had reportedly been foretold by one Prophetess Otom in 1770, almost 150 years before his birth. It is claimed that a blind female guest at his naming ceremony regained her sight when she held him in her arms and he looked into her eyes.

Merely aged five, Olumba began performing more magical feats. Approaching some women fetching water from a stream, he asked for water but did not present a cup. To the astonishment of onlookers, he gathered some leaves in his hands and magically transformed them into an enamel cup. After his blessing, the woman who offered him water was reportedly cured of fifteen years of barrenness.

In later years, Olumba progressed his miraculous feats to communicating with animals, and later his resuscitation of a dead monkey. He soon achieved the Lazarus standard of miracles resurrecting a man who had been shot dead and reviving a young slave maiden who had been worked to death on a farm. Olumba made no mention of the man's murderer or whether the slave girl was dejected to be brought back to continue life in servitude.

In life as much as in death, Olumba represented a mystic figure whose elusive persona continues to attract new converts. A cloud of mystery surrounds his death and the circumstances remain unclear with his funeral rites performed under secrecy. Since he insisted he was not born but 'manifested' onto earth, he vowed that he existed on multiple planes simultaneously and that his "jurisdiction stood above all elements of nature"[7] including death, rendering him immortal. Today, some followers insist Olumba is merely sleeping for the time being, while others claim he has ascended into heaven. In April 2000, Olumba

---

[7] Archive.org (2012) *His Physical Manifestation on Earth* leaderolumbaolumbaobuisalmightygod.org

bestowed his crown on his eldest son Rowland, whom he ordained as 'Christ, the King of Kings and the Lord of Lords.' His followers believe that for as long as Olumba's bloodline is at the helm of the movement, God is on earth. In life, Olumba never appeared in public beyond the grounds of the BCS headquarters at 34 Ambo Street in Calabar, Cross River State and his death in 2003 was not revealed until 2012. Even to this day, his passing has not been formally confirmed by his family. In the minds of many, he still reigns as king.

Lady Malaika

In the mid-2000s, residents of Mushin lived in fear of trespassing a particular corner of Alafia Street for it was the home of the mysterious Lady Malaika Agba. Little is known about her moment of prophetic realisation, as she claims to have existed in the world as God Almighty since birth. She styled herself as the creator of heaven, earth, and the oceans as well as the controller of the destiny of all beings on earth. She also claimed to defy the categories of gender, embodying both male and female forms psychologically. Born

Olayinka Oladipupo in Isolo, Lagos, she had ancestral links to the Ijebu region, the birthplace of her (earthly) parents.

Malaika's chosen title suggests she is the highest-ranking celestial being since *Agba* infers a senior status in Yorùbá, while her primary moniker alludes to an angelic nature. She established a house of worship named after the Holy Land near her home and as news of her self-professed gifts spread, she quickly amassed thousands of worshippers who called her 'Malaika Jesus' or *Baba* (father) and said prayers in her name. Capitalising on the almost equal split of Christians and Muslims in that part of Lagos, the architecture of her 'New Jerusalem Centre' was fashioned with iconic motifs from the Islamic and Christian traditions hosting both Friday prayers and Sunday worship, integrating the *Aladura* and Pentecostal style of fervent prayer and worship. A self-confessed hedonist, she was rumoured to keep a househusband as well as a number of virile young men as sexual submissives with changing frequency, such that local women pleaded with their husbands not to venture down Alafia Street for fear of being captivated by the prophetess.

Malaika's unorthodox spiritual practices included lashings of the whip for latecomers, disruptors and anyone caught falling asleep during her sermons. She was also known for an invasive procedure she deemed 'spiritual surgery' which led to at least one documented death. Three of Malaika's four children had died in infancy under mysterious circumstances and her adopted daughter Bose Olaniyi died suddenly aged twenty-one. On Malaika's instruction, a burial was hurriedly performed but Olaniyi's body was exhumed as police launched an investigation and an autopsy revealed the young woman had been injected with an unidentified substance.

Malaika's reign as a living goddess is notable because of the environment from which she emerged in a society notoriously hostile to women who stray from the established confines of womanhood. Malaika's claim to be the literal embodiment of God in human form also makes her distinct from other Nigerian women prophets who merely claim to be messengers. The criminal case synonymous with her name seemingly consigned her to a separate category of mental incapacitation, yet her devoted following did not demonstrate that she was perceived in that manner. Women suffering from mental retardation, far from being worshipped are often subject to societal abuse and exploitation. Blasphemous utterances such as her insistence of being *Olodumare* the Supreme Being at the very least would ordinarily be met with condemnation but with wit and charisma, Malaika eschewed those limitations, blazing a path not formerly trodden. Malaika came to national prominence after agreeing to be featured in an episode of the LTV 'strange but true' investigative series *Nkan Nbe*. Led by the broadcaster Kola Olawuyi, the feature examined the circumstances surrounding the sudden death and swift burial of the young woman linked to Malaika. Despite evidence of foul play and subsequent investigation by the CID, every lead in Olaniyi's case turned cold and the matter was laid to rest, giving Malaika free reign to continue her ministry.

Satguru Maharaj Ji

The self-styled 'Living Perfect Master' also known as the Black Jesus, 'Guru Maharaj Ji is another Nigerian messiah whose legend is awash with prophecy, miracle healing, rumours of ritual killings and the claim of the ultimate spiritual gift – the power of life over death. Born Mohammed Ibrahim in 1938, Maharaj Ji's encounter with the divine included a revelation of his new name and a mandate to 'liberate mankind from poverty, oppression and injustice.' The prophet locates his ministry within a commune set on a vast site along the Lagos-Ibadan highway known as the One Love Mission. The grounds are considered holy land and can only be treaded barefoot. Members adhere to strict conduct related to the performance of spiritual rites, modest clothing in approved colours, adherence to particular diets, enforced veganism, avoidance of alcohol, restriction of mobile communication devices and withdrawal from political participation. Maharaj Ji's fellowship borrows heavily from various religious traditions, particularly Hindu, from his Sanskrit name to the rites and rituals performed in his honour by followers. Appointed into his innermost circle are twelve disciples each in charge of managing various aspects of life for inhabitants of the commune.

Maharaj Ji has been known to offer spiritual counsel

to statesmen including General Ibrahim Babangida, Mohammed Abacha, and Hamza al-Mustapha. His influence among Nigeria's political elite was further demonstrated following his arrest for murder. In 1989 former followers of Maharaj Ji revealed to the press that 200 bodies were buried near the ashram on the site. The police assured the media of having investigated thoroughly yet failing to find any evidence. People recounted stories of family members setting off to the camp to seek miracles and healing but never returning. Accounts of buried bodies on the site were dismissed as rumours since they were unsubstantiated. Ten years later, the murder of a Ghanaian tourist by Maharaj Ji followers sparked a riot led by a coalition of local youths who stormed the site and torched the ashram, razing it to the ground. Maharaj Ji was charged and prosecuted for the crime but was acquitted in 2000 following a lengthy trial. Attempts to shut down the site by state agents from the opposition proved futile and Maharaj Ji returned to the helm to resume leadership of what had become a larger congregation. Now an octogenarian, the Living Perfect Master's claim of immortality is yet to be disproved.

CHAPTER 4

The magic of miracles

Christians have long maintained a complex relationship with magic, at once condemning witchcraft yet exalting inexplicable acts such as the parting of the Red Sea and the manifestation of manna from heaven. So magic is sanctioned in as much as it serves to benefit them exclusively and the gift remains in the hands of the chosen ones. Unlike sceptics who might apply cynicism to the plausibility of practical witchcraft, Christians who believe in the rebellion story of Lucifer are left to feel threatened by what they consider an abominable subversion of God's might, perceiving witchery as a crime against the Creator. As such, Christians are driven to antagonism since they fear that the intent of ungodly magic can only spell evil.

In Nigeria's deeply religious climate in which the world is perceived as a place awash with spirits, magical thinking, performed through either occultic means or prayers to God is a favoured recourse that allows practitioners regain a sense of control over challenging circumstances. Many are seduced by the repudiation of personal responsibility on offer, where the Devil is held responsible for any wrongdoing while achievements are attributed to God. This is not necessarily due to modesty, but because it posits adherents – in the eyes of others, as a person who is closer to God. An intoxicated driver can brazenly blame the Devil for an accident while doctors often profess to only 'care while God cures.' This expression is a commonplace feature on posters and stickers in many hospitals, which bizarrely serves to offer reassurance to patients since many believe that sin has a correlation with health.

Despite its seeming implausibility, it can be argued that there is power in faith since magic when performed collectively, has the potential to heal. A congruent gesture such as the laying of hands on the sick can give reassurance to the recipient, thus relieving anxiety which then can then extend into physical improvements in the patient. In the process, the short-lived placebo effect gained through magical miracles serves as confirmation to believers that supernatural factors are at play, further reinforcing the cycle.

Lewis (1986) offers a phenomenological analysis of magic arguing that "habit is unthinking," since failure to think removes the need to understand the causal factor responsible for an outcome. Citing the example of how people might not give much thought as to the mechanics of how aspirin helps to relieve headache given the overwhelming proof of efficiency, it is also likely that a person reliant on prayer miracles may be equally unconcerned about rationalising its process.

A 2008 (Nigerian) Sun newspaper headline read, *"Arrangee Miracle: Pastor arrested with fake electronic miracle machine."* The report was about an *arrangee* (dubious) pastor linked to Professor Peller who was said to have bestowed the preacher with practical magic skills and supernatural powers in a business deal bound by cash and the occult. In exchange for access to Peller's spirit medium, the unnamed pastor agreed to pay the magician ₦2 million[8] per year. Peller may have unusually broken the magician's oath to reveal his secrets, but the trickery in the deal laid in the preachers' belief that he had gained 'real' supernatural powers. Evidently, the Professor swindled the swindler. As the pastor raked in profits, Peller changed the terms of the agreement and demanded ₦10 million per annum. The preacher was reluctant to oblige, and their partnership soon fell apart. Not long afterwards, Peller was killed, and the minister who needed to maintain his reputation as a healer had to look to electronic gadgets to continue performing miracles. One of such devices was a static electricity generator worn by the performer and used to transmit current onto whomever they touched while the wearer remained unaffected. For an unsuspecting audience, the visual result created by the device was an unleashing of the Holy Ghost fire by the pastor onto a possessed person, which struck with a strong force that

---

[8] At the time of the magic miracle deal in the 1990s, one US dollar was exchangeable at the rate of approximately eight Nigerian naira, placing the sum at $250,000 p.a.

knocked them off their feet. As such, exorcisms became a staple of Sunday services and church members had become so accustomed to the deliverance routine that they would slump even before being touched, since failure to collapse could be read as a signifier of an evil spirit still residing within the person. Customarily, members who come forward to the pulpit for deliverance do not return to their seats until they have performed the slumping act of surrender, whether 'real' or feigned on their part.

A typical deliverance session would be structured to follow a big band style praise-worship segment of the service. Seamlessly blending song into prayer and speaking in tongues, at which point the pastor would take over the pulpit from the choirmaster. Drums, tambourines, and the keyboard will continue to amplify the prayers while the audience remains on their feet. Prayers will promise success in all aspects of life including health, business, finances, relationships, fertility, travel, and migration to lands of greener pastures but be followed by reminders that the Devil is also present in their midst and is actively seeking to stop people from receiving their blessings. The audience is often asked to jump and stomp their feet on the Devil's head vigorously. Viral videos have shown worshippers brutally whipping invisible demons, each armed with a *koboko*. Even without prompt, audiences often begin stomping as they assume prayer warrior mode.

While everyone present might be guaranteed a blessing, some special cases must be instigated by the pastor to demonstrate the full might of God. Strategic pauses between prayer points create moments in which audience members are free to interject the silence with spontaneous "hallelujahs" and cries of "I receive it" as they are bestowed with miracles. Many clasp their hands repeatedly to catch the blessings falling from heaven. Also to be expected is the sound of high-pitched hollering in which women would shriek and collapse as those around them come to their aid and usher them to the podium.

Deliverance services are predominantly attended by women, and since they have a higher predisposition to religiosity, are more likely to participate in spirited worship making them frequent subjects and co-performers of healing miracles. Although what happens on the pulpit might be viewed by outsiders as violating the body or intrusive of personal space, the social contract within the four walls of the church is such that a form of consent is presumed to have been given by the subject through raising their hands to be prayed upon, by shrieking or slumping and through their willingness to come forward to the stage.

As the special cases are lined up at the podium, the audience members, now sanctified and filled with their own blessings are asked to pray for their comrades in front by raising their hands in unison. The pastor begins to make revelatory declarations about the challenges and crisis each subject suffers. These can range from broad-ranging applies-to-almost-everyone utterances of "the Lord says your marriage is in danger, I pray for the spirit of unfaithfulness to release you," to more elaborate narratives with specific details about individuals, incurring gasps, bewilderment, ecstatic jumping and cries of "hallelujah, thank you, Jesus!"

Since music rests at the core of almost all expressions of spirituality, it is in many cases sacred to its rites and rituals. In Pentecostalism, music is central to invoking the divine and in its African form, it serves additional functions - preparation of one's self for the Spirit, and personal gratification. Pentecostals are peculiar in that they reject the tenets of earlier doctrines where religiosity was typically more communitarian than individualistic.

The notion of a personal relationship with Jesus is central to the heart of Pentecostal worship. Expressions of all-consuming love for Christ is confessed in deeply emotive songs such as Mercy Chinwo's *Excess Love* (2018) in which Jesus is venerated for making the ultimate sacrifice on the cross, for keeping promises even in death, for never lying, and for exhibiting unconditional love for unworthy souls. In Monique's *Power Flow* (2014) the worshipper confesses their expectation of signs and wonders, as witnessed in the days when Moses parted the Red Sea. A resurrection is staged in the music video to be taken either literally or as a metaphor for the boundless possibilities of what faith can do. Ada Ehi's *Only You Jesus* (2016) is a compelling miracle-inducing prayer song featuring extensive glossolalia (speaking in tongues) ad-libs. The accompanying video for the track about the enduring power of the resurrected Christ to heal the sick and raise the dead depicts dramatic scenes that would not be amiss in a Nollywood flick, ensuring its chart-topping success.

Megachurches in Lagos such as Chris Oyakhilome's Christ Embassy and its music arm Loveworld Records kickstarted the careers of Ehi and other gospel singers such as Sinach, Joe Praize, and Eben. Churches routinely draw in large crowds by inviting popular artists to their stages. *Fuji* music icon Pasuma courted controversy when he was billed to perform at a Redeemed Christian Church of God (RCCG) crusade in 2015. But the furore was not about whether or not Pasuma had a place on the pulpit alongside actors, comedians and other secular artists - rather the conflict was presented by his faith as a practising Muslim. Although Islam and Pentecostalism have historically experienced a complex convergence in the south of Nigeria, its manifestation was not (yet) such that a notoriously worldly character like Pasuma could be accommodated. The incident generated public debate about the evolution of the Pentecostal stage as a site of entertainment.

For women and girls living in largely repressive

patriarchal communities, opportunities to redress or subvert the power balance are often possible only through collective action. Spiritual gatherings provide an antidote by presenting an opportunity for women to negotiate a form of subconscious collective bargaining where bodily expressions are temporarily exempt from policing. In the context of spirit possession, women are able to manifest behaviours and perform in states of undress that would have otherwise come under scrutiny outside the church. Thus, their willingness to partake in miracle performance is driven not only by collective frenzy, but as a temporary means of mitigating repressive cultural limitations.

The phenomenon of women miracle performers can also be viewed with a reverse understanding of conversion disorder where mental distress is converted into physical aches and pains that cannot be explained by medical evaluation. Conversion disorder might take the form of paralysis or loss of vision after witnessing horrific incidents. So rather than an inability to function with body parts that have experienced trauma, miracle performers charged with adrenaline are seemingly able to galvanise immobile body parts into action. These feats are then evidenced as miracles, although they are almost always short-lived.

American scientific sceptic James Randi retired from a distinguished career in magic to investigate and debunk supernatural claims made by spiritualists with his findings detailed in the 1987 publication *The Faith Healers*. Examining the claims made by evangelists A.A. Allen, Ernest Angley, Willard Fuller, WV Grant, Oral Roberts, Pat Robertson, and Ralph DiOrio, Randi exposed the use of trickery and sleight of hand techniques used to perform miracles. The most amusing revelation came from Peter Popoff's TV exposé, where Randi attended one of his miracle crusades to unmask the evangelist's reliance on the word-for-word cues he was being fed via wireless radio transmission about ailments members had written on their prayer cards. The disclosure crippled Popoff's faith healing career and he plummeted from enjoying annual earnings of $4 million to declaring bankruptcy.

Larry Skelton, an associate of Popoff for twenty-five years admitted in 2017; "When you're praying for the sick, it's through the Holy Spirit, and sometimes it works freely, and then there are other times when the Spirit is just not there. On the days when the Holy Spirit didn't show up freely, you had to help it along."[9]

Randi's infamous *One Million Dollar Paranormal Challenge,* a pledge offered to anyone who could demonstrate supernatural ability under scientific testing remained unclaimed throughout its fifty-year lifespan, despite more than one thousand attempts. Since the first paranormal challenge by the Scientific American magazine in 1922 of which Harry Houdini served as an investigator, there have been more than forty global challenges with a total prize value exceeding $2 million. In almost a hundred years, no participants have been able to demonstrate supernatural ability under scientific examination.

While there is a plethora of evidence for fraudulent practices performed on the pulpit, the willingness of audiences to participate in miracle performance is often overlooked. Many among magician's audiences understand that illusions are carefully executed crafts of trickery yet some will assign supernatural ability to

---

[9] GQ. Oppenheimer, M. (2017). *Peter Popoff, the Born-Again Scoundrel*

the showmen as a way of rationalising what they witnessed. Miracle seekers go a step further by becoming the subjects of the illusion, taking pride in performing it and thereby presenting themselves as special in that they have been touched by God. Some may utilise the performance as a form of visualisation and precursor to the impending miracle while others succumb to group hypnosis.

American evangelist Kathryn Kuhlman was famous for her healing crusades between the 1940s and 70s amassing a television audience of millions around the world. Her weekly televised program *I Believe in Miracles* was aired internationally and in her thirty-year career, an estimated two million people reported they had been healed by her. Kuhlman admitted to having little theological knowledge but claimed to possess the gift of healing and published a biography detailing what she claims were medically documented healings, generating debates about the authenticity of her ministry. In the late 1960s, researcher William A. Nolen produced a case study of twenty-three people who claimed to have been healed by Kuhlman but when followed up, he discovered that there were no lasting cures in any of the cases.

During one of Kuhlman's crusades, a woman undergoing treatment for cancer on her spine had dramatically removed her back brace and ran across the stage to demonstrate her healing to the stadium-sized audience. The next day the woman's spine collapsed, and she died four months later. Nolen's findings on the longevity of Kuhlman's healings were refuted by her followers who dismissed the sample size of the research as insufficient. Kuhlman is considered as instrumental to the present-day American Pentecostal movement alongside another woman preacher Aimee Semple MacPherson, who founded the Foursquare Church, which has a significant presence in Nigeria.

In 1974 Nolen published *Healing: A Doctor in Search of a Miracle* detailing his quest to examine faith healers over a two-year period. He concluded that no patients with an organic disease had been cured and that psychic surgery relied on magic and sleight of hand trickery, uncovering many cases of fraud.

Church as stage: Nollywood on the Pulpit

Of the many parallels to be drawn between Nollywood and Pentecostalism, the fall out between Jim Iyke and TB Joshua not only represents the increasing convergence of the two industries but spontaneous performance in action. Nollywood bad boy Iyke had enjoyed a cult status for decades, effortlessly exuding a cool, hip, irreverent demeanour like the roles he often played on screen. As one of the highest-paid actors in the industry, he has appeared in more than 160 films and is a Taekwondo Black Belt. In 2013, he became desperate for a miracle that could alleviate his mother's deteriorating health. He visited Joshua's megachurch for the first time with an entourage comprised of his sister, a personal assistant and a bodyguard and together they watched the live-stream service from a corner of the auditorium. With a comfortable distance away from the stage, Iyke later recalled laughing at the animated gestures of people falling over as Joshua laid hands on them during the deliverance service. Iyke said his sister casually reprimanded him and dared him to go to the podium if he really thought it was all a show. Her provocation combined with his concern about their mother's health made him take on the challenge and they headed for the pulpit. The superstar actor was immediately recognised as people cleared his path to the stage. The audience gasped and watched in shock as the televangelist took complete control of Iyke. Years later, Iyke feigned amnesia claiming that from the moment Joshua's hands touched him, he remembers nothing until he came around again after the deliverance.

Captured on camera and broadcast to a live audience of millions, an entity seemingly spoke from within Iyke revealing the Devil's desire to destroy him. The evil spirit also confessed that it was responsible for Iyke's failed relationships and inability to find a wife. The utterances were not unlike what would be heard by possessed souls as priests laid hands on them in a Mount Zion film. A dazed Iyke flung off his shoes as stagehands struggled to keep him on his feet. Having regained his composure, Iyke said his actions on the stage had been 'embarrassing.' He coyly embraced his sister, sobbing into her arms, shying away from the cameras as though he wished he could disappear.

Unsurprisingly, Iyke's film career suffered and in interviews that followed, he claimed not to have an explanation of how the dramatic deliverance was performed on him, leaving him convinced he had been tricked by the preacher – the real showman. Many wondered if Iyke had been hypnotised by Joshua leaving his subconscious mind to perform learned behaviour. Fans asked how the too-cool-for-school actor found himself in the position of those he had mocked. Some observers concluded that Iyke was probably performing a well-paid role contracted by Joshua, but both parties underestimated the damage to Iyke's career and subsequently fell out. That assertion would mean that the church is perceived as just another form of showbusiness.

In contrast to the Iyke-Joshua fall out, a sweet alliance was forged between Nollywood prodigal son Ernest Asuzu and megachurch leader Prophet Jeremiah Fufeyin. Although never quite landing leading roles like Iyke, actor and rapper Asuzu was similarly typecast in bad-boy roles and is a familiar face to audiences with appearances in more than fifty films including *Rituals* (1997) and *Living Abroad* (2004). At the peak of his career, the actor declared he was quitting the 'evil' Nollywood industry only to re-emerge a decade later begging shirtless on the streets of Lagos. Fans quickly gathered around him with their phones recording the event. Asuzu revealed his desperation was due to a series of health issues which began after a spiritual attack where an invisible woman slapped his face. When the footage went viral, he was invited to receive healing at Fufeyin's Mercyland Deliverance Ministry.

Taking centre stage, Asuzu appeared with his wife who confirmed the actor had suffered a stroke and was unable to walk unaided. The prophet massaged the actor's knee with anointing oil and he immediately began to walk. Jeremiah also presented the couple with a cash gift of ₦1.5million (£3,000), an SUV and a new home in Lagos all captured in high definition for Mercyland TV. Once again, the actor assumed his hip-hop persona 'El Cream' and released a single in 2017 which was sponsored by the church. In return, the actor occasionally referenced the prophet in social media posts over a two-year period. Both parties subsequently parted ways quietly and amicably.

Actors in Nollywood have been known to make appearances in megachurches although never quite in the vein of Iyke's dramatic episode. RCCG, one of the leading churches of the *Aladura*-Pentecostal variety which boasts a robust presence in 190 countries in the world, has a membership of fourteen million in Nigeria alone, with an average of 100,000 people attending its weekly Sunday service. RCCG is led by Enoch Adeboye, whose net worth is estimated at $130 million. In 2011, a special Nollywood event was commissioned which saw a rota of key figures attend the sermon themed *'Success in Life Requires Something Supernatural.'* The event was designed to impart wisdom and offer prayers for the performers who in turn were expected to reciprocate generously in the thanksgiving ceremony. Industry figures in attendance included producer Wale Adenuga as well as actors Jide Kosoko, Segun Arinze, Justus Esiri, and Mike Bamiloye, whose work is explored in Chapter 6.

The art of mythmaking

Of Nigeria's array of messiahs and prophets, Benson Idahosa is often singled out as an influential figure central to the roots of Nigerian Pentecostalism. The claim might be due to his sheer proficiency at mythmaking, as numerous scholars refer to him as 'the father of Pentecostalism in Nigeria' for being the country's first Pentecostal archbishop and televangelist. Born in Benin City in 1938, he was said to have suffered from health complications which resulted in his parents abandoning him to die at a rubbish site. But at the moment his mother almost deserted him, a sign from heaven in the form of thunder, lightning and torrential rainfall convinced her of his gift and she returned home with him. As a teenager, he encountered a man of God who converted him to Christ. He soon sought out subjects for miracles that would demonstrate his divine calling. Aged twenty-four, he claimed to have wandered through the streets of his hometown looking for a corpse to revive. He found a recently deceased girl being prepared for burial and brought her back to life by uttering her name and the commandment; "Arise in the name of the Lord Jesus Christ!" A week later, it was the turn of an eight-year-old boy to become undead. During one sermon Idahosa claimed to have spiritually intercepted a plan by an alliance of all the world's witches and wizards to stage an international conference in Nigeria.[10]

The Idahosa legend often told by Nigerians is the story of how Aliko Dangote (currently the wealthiest black person in the world) experienced a change of fortune after an encounter with the archbishop. Idahosa had supposedly prophesied and prayed for the Nigerian businessman (now worth $14 billion) declaring, "the world will get up for you." The 'getting up' was a literal and metaphorical reference to an extraordinary chain of events in which a young Dangote gave up his seat on a US-bound plane for Idahosa's guest in an altruistic gesture.

According to one devotee Michael Reid, a British evangelist and modern-day missionary, Idahosa's supernatural powers were again proven when a witchdoctor disrupted one of his conventions by

---

[10] The Nigerian Voice (2012) *Archbishop Benson Idahosa: The Error and Falsehood of Ex-Olumba Olumba Pastor's Confession*. Thenigerianvoice.com

divining a heavy downpour of rain. The troublemaker allegedly dropped dead within the hour the bishop willed it so. The grandest assertion associated with Idahosa is a resurrection bonanza in which he claimed to have brought eight dead people back to life. The claim had originated within Idahosa's camp but failed to gain traction outside Nigeria. Idahosa first made the claim on the pulpit while preaching at Benny Hinn Ministries in Texas and proceeded onto a tour of the UK but he was warned by promoters that his resurrection claims could not be made in Britain as the Advertising Standards Authority requested proof of death in all the cases. With none provided, all the claims were dropped.[11]

In the years that followed, a number of Idahosa's protégés such as David Oyedepo and Chris Oyakhilome became figureheads of the Pentecostal movement in Nigeria. Leadership rivalry was commonplace in the industry and to claim spiritual supremacy over their counterparts, incredible stories were leaked to the press or recounted as testimonies

---

[11] Guardian (2000). *Sects, power and miracles in the Bible belt of Essex.* Theguardian.com

during sermons. RCCG's leader Enoch Adeboye remarkably claims to have driven for two hundred miles on an empty fuel tank with an engine presumably powered by the blood of Jesus. This was followed by another claim of breakfast with God during which they both drank tea, a surreal encounter reminiscent of the biblical Enoch's walk with God in the Book of Genesis. In their efforts to convince unbelievers, church members attest to the miracle claims as if they were eyewitnesses to the occurrences. Recounted continuously, the fantastical stories become difficult to challenge. For example, T.B. Joshua's mythmaking dates back to even before he was born, with self-prophesied claims that his birth had been foretold one hundred years prior. He claimed to have lived in his mother's womb for fifteen months and cheated death in a bomb explosion at just one week old.

Like the seven tales of miraculous births in the Bible, Pentecostal prophets are often believed to have entered the world amidst extraordinary circumstances. Moses Orimolade Tunolase founder of the uniform compliant 'white garment' wearing church Cherubim and Seraphim claimed his divine abilities were first witnessed by his mother while he was still in her womb. It is claimed that in a moment of distress while struggling with firewood she had gathered in the forest, she found herself unable to manage the heavy load with no one around to help. Suddenly a voice spoke to her saying, "Do not be frightened, I am the child in your womb." She found she was able to lift the logs with the help of the mystic force. To quench any doubt about the incident, it was further claimed that Tunolase began walking on the same day he was born. His parents feared the societal repercussions of the anomaly and instructed a herbalist to take away his strength and render him a cripple. Tunolase came to be revered as a saint by his followers. Even in death, the legend of Saint Moses Tunolase continues to spread. On his prior instruction, his grave was exhumed for observation forty years after his death and eyewitnesses allegedly noted his body's lack of decay or blemish as he had foretold.

Also operating on a self-mythologising backstory, the infamous 'Lady Apostle' Helen Ukpabio claims to have broken free from the occult, witchcraft and Satanism, having been groomed since her teenage years to wed the Prince of Darkness himself. On receiving the call of God, her acquired gifts include dominion over the Devil and she established her church with a commitment to casting out demons and marine spirits in the form of witches and mermaids - a biography that established her as a foremost authority on witchcraft, rapidly amassing millions of global followers.

Conversion mythology such as Paul's encounter with the divine on the road to Damascus is also commonplace. Apostle Suleman of Omega Fire Ministries was born a Muslim but is claimed to have been destined to be a prophet of Christ since birth. It is said that his mother was visited in his birthplace of Benin by prophets of God from Warri who declared her new-born child a future minister of the gospel. Despite his Islamic upbringing, Suleman eventually found his way to the church and is today one of Nigeria's leading televangelists. Suleman is famed for his prophetic declarations which his followers take pride in as evidence of his calling. He often makes predictions on highly probable occurrences that fail to impress many outside his camp. Some of these include predictions that some of the Chibok girls kidnapped by

Boko Haram militants would fall pregnant, Nigeria's 75-year-old president would struggle with his health, wildfire would engulf parts of America, Donald Trump would move the US Embassy in Israel from Tel Aviv to Jerusalem, Britain would be struck by a terror attack and that a new crop of Nollywood stars would emerge. Remarkably, Suleman also predicted that in 2016, God would disgrace all 'diabolical pastors' in Nigeria, lest anyone mistake him for a charlatan.

Joshua's SCOAN church in Lagos attracts 50,000[12] worshippers each week, with many travelling as far afield as South Africa to witness him in action, a mark of success which has not gone unnoticed on the scene. His rival Okotie had once claimed that Joshua received his healing powers through the Satanist Olumba Olumba, an incredibly damaging charge. Agina (2010) alleges that of such claims, "there is no smoke without fire" and went further into mapping the links between so-called Devil-worship and success in Pentecostal leadership. Citing a 2009 Punch newspaper headline

[12] The Guardian. Mark, M. (2013). *Lagos businesses cash in on lure of super-pastor TB Joshua.* Theguardian.com

Gruesome Murder in the Name of God, Agina recalls the murder of a twelve-year-old girl by the pastors of a Cherubim and Seraphim church in Osun State where they sacrificed the girl to the Devil in a bid to attract more members to the church.

In recent times, spats between Pentecostal leaders have become as commonplace as Twitter beefs between rappers generating impassioned social media responses from fans and followers each eagerly defending their side. From Peller Jnr vs Joshua and Oyakhilome, Okotie vs Joshua, Oyakhilome vs Ashimolowo, Ashimolowo vs Odumeje, to Adelaja vs Adeboye,[13] accusations of false prophesy abound.

Jesu Oyingbo, Jesus of Ikot-Ekpene, Olumba Olumba Obu, Benson Idahosa and the unlikely Professor Peller had laid the blueprints and strategies for a new wave of charismatic leadership that would transform the nature of Afro-Pentecostalism forever.

---

[13] Daily Post Odunsi, W, (2017) Adeboye is a liar, misinterprets Bible – Pastor Adelaja carpets RCCG head. Dailypost.ng

Resurrection: the ultimate miracle

In February 2019, Alph Lukau the Congolese founder of a popular megachurch near Johannesburg orchestrated an extraordinary scene he had hoped would make him a global name in the cut-throat Pentecostal scene. Claims of resurrection miracles by African Pentecostals date back to the early 1920s but few have been staged for live audiences since the proliferation of recording devices. The most recent resurrection claim by a Pentecostal figure was made by Samuel Oshoffa in Nigeria in 1976, a feat which was just one of his many professed resurrections. The first took place in 1947 after he experienced a divine revelation while wandering through a desolate forest during a solar eclipse. His church quickly earned its place as a major contender among Nigeria's *Aladura* churches. At the time of his death in 1985, Oshoffa's Celestial Church of Christ had a membership of 3.1 million people[14] and today more than five per cent of the population of the Republic of Benin are Celestials.

---

[14] Statistics from Barrett, Kurian, Johnson (2001)

Both Apostle Suleman and Shepherd Bushiri have in recent years broadcasted resurrection feats online, but their subjects were recently deceased children thought to have been revived within minutes of death and neither had been formally pronounced dead.

Lukau had made an impression to some degree by sharing curated images of his luxurious fleet of cars and private jets with his Instagram followers with 500,000 subscribers watching his live stream miracle services on YouTube. He had established a track record of healing the eternally damned which according to him include homosexuals, adult bedwetters, adulterous wives, sex workers, witches and 'husband snatchers.' His miracle repertoire highlighted in provocative viral videos tagged with titles such as *"Hairdresser bewitches client to snatch her husband,"* and *"Former prostitute gets engaged in church"* had amassed millions of views. In keeping up with their shared audience base, Nollywood films uploaded to YouTube in recent times completely do away with their formal titles which are replaced by salacious summaries of the plot such as *"My driver gives it to me till I can't walk"* accompanied by graphic thumbnails from sex scenes.

Lukau's wish for global fame would be fulfilled, but for all the wrong reasons. The congregation at that Sunday's service had already witnessed performances of incredible feats which saw the lame throw away their wheelchairs after Lukau laid hands on them. As he prayed in tongues, a woman stormed into the church urgently alerting the preacher to "something happening outside." In the street, a hearse carrying a coffin had been disturbed and the vehicle was surrounded by wailing mourners. People purporting to be relatives of the deceased recounted stories of the dead man's brief illness in the preceding days and his sudden death. The congregation reconvened outside, and cameras and phones were whipped out to capture the spectacle. This was Lukau's moment. He ordered for the casket to be opened and inside laid a young man dressed in a white suit. Lukau sought confirmation that the man had been dead for three days. Commanding silence amidst the chaos, he asked onlookers to lift up their hands in prayer and like Jesus at the tomb of Lazarus he commanded; "Elliot, rise up!" The man in the casket sat up and looked around him, dazed. "The coffin is empty" Lukau declared, and the crowd screamed for joy. With strategically positioned cameras on hand to document the miracle, Lukau led the resurrected man onto the church stage.

As videos and images from the incredible scene spread, so did loose ends and plot holes in the narrative. The company that loaned out the hearse and the coffin denied knowledge of a funeral but instead insisted they had supplied the goods for theatrical use, absolving themselves of complicity.[15] Neighbours of the resurrected man had seen him leave home for church earlier that morning. Social media users identified him as the recipient of a previous wheelchair miracle and soon it became evident that the event was staged, and few could defend Lukau. Fellow preachers fearing the backlash against the miracle healing industry joined in to denounce Lukau for "bringing Christianity into disrepute." Curiously, the loudest of these critics was fellow South Africa based evangelist Paseka Motsoeneng also known as Prophet Mboro who challenged Lukau to prove his might by resurrecting Nelson Mandela. Critics noted that

---

[15] BBC News. (2019). *Undertakers to sue over fake resurrection.* Bbc.co.uk

Mboro, founder of the Church of Incredible Happenings had also boasted of improbable feats and was rumoured to have made claims about visiting heaven and charging followers to reveal pictures.[16] At the time, Mboro's stunt had opened the floodgates as the following year saw Zimbabwean preacher Paul Sanyangore make global headlines for a stunt in which he placed a phone call to heaven from the pulpit. Interceding in prayer on behalf of a woman, he relayed intimate facts that God had told him about her before he declared her healed.[17] Another prophet, Shepherd Bushiri followed by staging a levitation miracle depicting him walking on air with video effects too poor even for old Nollywood. Nonetheless, Bushiri is one of Africa's wealthiest preachers and his New Years' Eve conventions regularly fill out the FNB Stadium, a 95,000-capacity arena in Johannesburg. In gift shops at such events, sanctified goods outsell Bibles and hymnbooks. Pentecostal paraphernalia on

[16] BBC News. (2016). *South African preacher mocked after charging for 'heavenly' photos*. Bbc.co.uk

[17] The Times Aislinn Laing, J. (2017). *Zimbabwean pastor 'talks to God on his mobile phone.'* Thetimes.co.uk

display often include anointed umbrellas to ward off thunder and lighting, *'Do as I say'* anointing oil, *'Leave my man alone'* oil or pheromones marketed as *'Love me and marry me'* perfume.

In a cruel twist of fate, Lukau's lead actor in the resurrection stunt known as Elliot aka Thabiso Mlanje died shortly after the event. Following media interest and calls for criminal prosecution, Elliot fled South Africa to his native Zimbabwe, where an underlying illness was triggered. He was confirmed by police to have died from complications relating to pneumonia aged 28. He was not resurrected.

Not just healing but permanent healing

In October 2019, an anonymous Nigerian woman with a deformity in her upper right arm appeared in a series of viral videos depicting her jaw-dropping miracle healing. In each setting, the woman demonstrated the ability to lengthen her dislocated arm which initially appeared boneless due to a suspected case of Ehlers-Danlos Syndrome, allowing her to contort the affected body parts. In different churches, she was singled out by preachers as the would-be recipient of a special miracle. Various degrees of performativity accompanied each event as the preachers elongated her squashed arm and astonished onlookers hurled out cash offerings crying out for their turn. As clips were shared online, a pattern soon unfolded, and the miracle was revealed as a scam. The pastors were ruthlessly ridiculed for the staged miracles but the preacher with the greatest clout among them - Dr Chris Okafor, the prophet of the Mountain of Liberation and Miracle Ministry insisted on defending his position. Audaciously, Okafor claimed that the woman's ailment was of a spiritual nature and recurrent because of her inability to commit to a particular church. More so, the healing he offered was the most powerful and lasting.

Journalist Chris Kehinde Nwandu tracked down the woman and identified her as Bose Olasunkanmi. In her interview, she echoed Okafor claiming that her mysterious illness always returned after each healing ceremony and as such, she would visit a new church in hope of a permanent solution. She feigned ignorance of her medical diagnosis and denied receiving payment from any of the preachers. Following the revelation, membership at Okafor's 'Liberation City' increased exponentially.

Failed miracle missions

The tendency to utilise magical tropes in miracle performance has long been prevalent in Nigeria, leaving today's key players with a playbook of tried and tested methods to employ or avoid. In 1991, one Prophet Daniel Abodunrin arrived in a long robe at the zoological garden of the University of Ibadan and requested to be let into a caged enclosure that housed their big cats. A crowd gathered as he declared his intention to prove that the God of the biblical Daniel was still alive, and that he would save him just like he sent an angel to close the jaws of the lions in the den. It is not clear how access was granted but eyewitnesses recall Abodunrin entering the cage armed with a Bible, reciting verses and calling out to the God of Daniel for deliverance. At first, the crowd gasped as the lions retreated but the prophet inched closer and louder towards them as he prayed, summoning angels to descend and shut the mouths of the lions. Agitated, the cornered lions pounced on him, devouring his flesh. Only Abodunrin's head and his tattered Bible could be recovered. Abodunrin's failed miracle mission divided opinion as his devotees contended that the lions were possessed by evil spirits and should be slaughtered.

Though contemporary Christian scholars largely dispute the existence of the biblical Daniel, the retelling of his story often places emphasis on his miraculous deliverance in the lion's den. Less is revealed about Daniel's proficiency in magic, overlooking the fact that he was a diviner and was designated the chief of magicians, enchanters, and soothsayers in the court of King Nebuchadnezzar and later Darius the Mede. Even as folklore, Daniel's triumph in the den had more to it than merely being found 'blameless' before God and he may have owed his survival to his mystical prowess.

Other failed miracle missions recorded in Africa include an event in which a prophet sought to restage Jesus' walk on water by attempting the stunt on crocodile-infested waters with a plan to use the reptiles as steppingstones. Instead, he was eaten by three crocodiles as his followers watched helplessly.[18] In another event, a self-proclaimed messiah who had hoped to attain David Blaine's status died of starvation. American illusionist and endurance artist Blaine famously pulled off a forty-four-day fast while confined in a glass box whereas Khulu Manyuka, aka Jesus of Zimbabwe died while attempting the stunt.[19]

Pentecostal pandemic

The devastation of COVID-19 on the world in early 2020 may come to signify a turning point in the Pentecostal business as time reveals the lasting ramifications of the pandemic. Worldwide, churches shut their doors to curb the spread of the virus and preachers finetuned accessibility of their online platforms for receiving offerings and donations electronically. Many ramped up their online streaming with subscription models and pay-per-view access for live Zoom prayer sessions collecting payments through

---

[18] Christian Post. Gotera, J. (2017) *Pastor Tries to imitate Jesus's miracle of walking on water - but gets devoured by 3 crocodiles* Christianpost.com
[19] Premier Christian News. Tooley, H. (2015) *Khulu Reinfirst Manyuka dies after trying to imitate Jesus* Premierchristian.news

cash apps and PayPal. In the Middle East, pilgrimage tours to Jerusalem came to a halt, Mecca shut its gates, and elsewhere Catholics suspended communion and holy water use. In Rio de Janeiro, the Christ the Redeemer monument was digitally re-robed in medical scrubs (see fig. 1) in an artistic intervention. More than ever before, the giant statue's outstretched arms signified the reassurance the world needed. It seemed all eyes were on science for answers, not on God. Faith healers like everybody else appeared to be waiting for coronavirus to be subdued to be able to get back to work.

Some could not resist capitalising on the pandemic, marketing Corona-banishing ointments for sale. Bishop Climate Wiseman of the Kingdom Church in south London packaged 100ml bottles of olive oil tied with pieces of red yarn branding them 'plague protection kits' for sale at almost £100 each. Wiseman soon found himself under investigation by the UK Charity Commission.[20] Across the Atlantic, Jim Bakker pleaded for donations to avoid filing for bankruptcy

---

[20] BBC News (2 April 2020) *Coronavirus: London church investigated over 'protection oil'* Bbc.co.uk

after he was fined for selling bogus coronavirus cures for $80 each.[21] Televangelist Kenneth Copeland urged viewers to continue paying tithes and offerings despite unemployment.

Unsurprisingly all the pre-2020 predictions made from Pentecostal pulpits in the previous year omitted any mention of the pandemic, but many prophets were quick to make pronouncements that largely chimed with the official consensus. Notably, many were vehemently opposed to excessive governmental imposition on personal freedoms. At least thirty cases of US pastors who succumbed to coronavirus were reported in April. Across America's Bible Belt, the tragedies hit hard particularly among black Pentecostal groups following a message of defiance against government mandates banning group gatherings. Bishop Gerald Glenn who declared; "God is larger than this virus" later died of COVID-19 in Virginia.[22]

As the world resettles into changing modes of the new normal, time will tell the extent to which the

---

[21] The Independent (24 April 2020) *'A phantom plague': America's Bible Belt played down the pandemic and even cashed in. Now dozens of pastors are dead* Independent.co.uk

[22] Sky News (14 April 2020) *Coronavirus: US pastor who said 'God is larger than this virus' and defied social distancing dies of COVID-19* News.sky.com

pandemic will disrupt the sector, as fewer people return to packed auditoriums in reverence of preachers who failed them at their darkest hour. Many will likely consider themselves lucky or blessed to have survived the epidemic and will return for that reason alone. Counter movements organised to tackle religious exploitation in Nigeria through critical thinking such as the *#FreeTheSheeple* movement led by Ifedayo Olarinde have amassed greater traction online in the wake of the pandemic.

Miracle performances like Lukau's poorly executed Lazarus re-enactment, Sanyangore's telephone call to heaven, Mboro's tour of the celestial city, and Okafor's permanent healing are now routinely mocked, amplified by the meme culture of the digital age.

Many observers denounce these men as charlatans and false prophets, yet simultaneously hold on to the belief that 'true prophets' exist. In turn, followers of those maligned as false prophets argue that all true prophets including Christ were disparaged as false prophets in their time. Therefore, the refusal of the masses to believe in their chosen prophet in itself is evidence of their ordination.

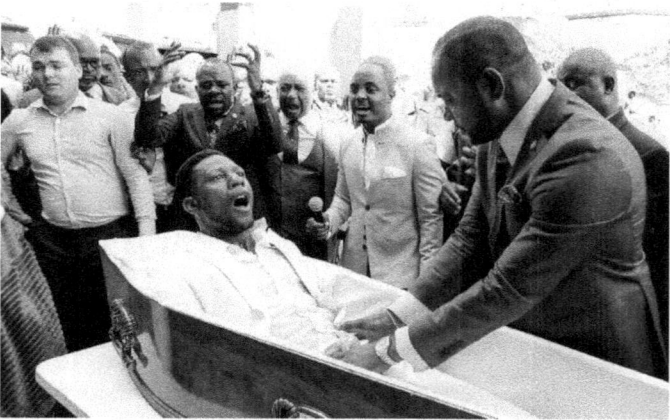

Alph Lukau performing a resurrection miracle in February 2019
Image © Alleluia Ministries International

CHAPTER 5

Pentecostal theatrics

Today there are 600 million Pentecostals in the world with thirty-five per cent of them located in sub-Saharan Africa.[23] In Nigeria, a nation with the seventh-largest population in the world estimated at 200 million, religion is big business. Many would-be preachers are attracted to the non-denominational structure of Pentecostalism where ordination merely requires self-declaration of the call of God, bypassing

---

[23] Pew Research Centre (2011) *Christian movements and Denominations.* Pewforum.org

years otherwise spent in clergy training. As such, entrepreneurship in the field is fiercely competitive with every street corner overflowing with a surplus of churches.

The Pentecostal experience is marked primarily by performativity as well as praise worship and prayer – (the latter is explored in Chapter 7). Local recruitment is strongly reliant on posters and leaflets, with audiences far afield allured by viral social media clips, as each latest release aims to elicit greater audience response. Billboards and posters for services are not unlike that of Nollywood, laden with detail rather than intrigue. Some have included machete-wielding pastors prepared to wage spiritual battles with the Devil and others strapped with piles of cash promising to eradicate financial burdens. (See fig. 2 - 7)

Along with new film releases, pop music concerts and political campaigns, Pentecostals are competing in the marketplace of culture for their share of audiences and therefore persuasion is key. The movement's embrace of mass media in its crudest form has given it more prominence, visibility and influence in comparison to its competitors in the religious market.

Dyrness (2001) examined the shift from austere imagery favoured by Protestants, with emphasis on nature – flowers, streams, meadows, and green hills, in contrast to the Pentecostal tendency to borrow from popular culture, modelling their campaigns after political billboards in which confident leaders assure voters of their capability.

The medium of television for evangelism has also been key in expanding the reach of megachurches, with millions of members and branches in every corner of the globe. Since internet access is not as readily available in rural areas, television remains a popular medium for recruitment and continues to prove useful for evangelicals.

Nigerian Pentecostals can be said to have brought their business acumen and zeal for the gospel into transforming Pentecostalism into a global movement. They have utilised every medium of communication to attract and keep audiences maintaining profitable operations. Rather than the imposition of dogma on followers, its members are drawn to it as it reflects their dispositions, aspirations and beliefs as each preacher carves out his own niche within the industry.

Theatrics was adopted by the medieval church to elaborate key events in the gospels when marking crucial festivities, but Pentecostal leaders have re-appropriated it to dazzle audiences. Among emerging young preachers, some have been more blatant about challenging the notion of what the twenty-first-century church can be.

Utilising Nollywood's melodramatic trope as a framework, Pentecostal theatrics can be read through its key players; the flamboyant preachers, charismatic women worshippers, camp men in the choir, and not least its audiences, looking at how each negotiates the space within the church, commanding authority and wielding power through performance.

Prophet Chukwuemeka Ohanaemere aka Odumeje takes his strategy straight out of the WWE playbook. The ultimate form of live entertainment, television wrestling combines bravado and athletic proficiency with well-timed illusions performed in sync with opponents in a series of actions that only reach a crescendo when audience frenzy peaks. This approach has made Prophet Chukwu's Holy Ghost Intervention Ministry one of the most popular venues in Anambra.

Designating himself the Devil-fighting stage name of *Liquid Metal* aka *Odumeje the Lion*, he is known for his unorthodox methods in combating demons. Doing away with the strait-laced suit and tie, Odumeje steps onto the stage in tight sports vests showing off his lean physique and six-pack abs. Rather than begin the service, this champion priest prefers to arrive only after the auditorium is full, entering to thunderous ovation. Flanked by bodyguards as he jogs to the stage, his followers chant his name jubilantly. His church sermons featuring combatant deliverance segments are emceed by a domineering commentator who narrates the action ringside style. On YouTube, he can be seen in his element restoring vision to the blind, healing gangrene, cancer, infertility, mental illness, and even one case of poverty. His subjects of choice for takedowns have included women but are often muscular young men seemingly outweighing him who are impressively smacked-down in undefended moves.

In stark contrast to his contemporaries, Odumeje's stage presence is striking in that he seems to perform with self-awareness about his place in the broader context of Pentecostal theatrics. He appears keen to draw on the familiarity of television wrestling, utilising iconic props such as breakable folding chairs - yet he emphasises that in the context of the church, he is covering new ground. When he is not speaking in tongues, he is often heard declaring; "I don't do shows, I don't do movies, this is all real!" In one viral video he lays hands on a man, placing him into a trancelike state, lifting him up, spinning and throwing him into rows of unoccupied plastic chairs. All the while, the frantic MC exclaims; "This is a supernatural man operating in the midst of natural men – DON'T TRY THIS AT HOME!" Odumeje continues to be a sensation in Onitsha where his showstopping sermons attract thousands weekly. He is the first prophet to publicly sign a talent representation and management deal with a public relations company. He maintains topicality through various actions such as collaborations with secular hip-hop artists or cash giveaway events. In one instance, he announced his plans to stage a mass-resurrection event, but local government chiefs conveniently imposed a ban on miracle performances at all mortuaries and hospitals, making him (almost) able to claim the feat without even trying.

But Odumeje is just one of many among Nigeria's superstar prophets. Prophet Jeremiah of Mercyland, aka the 'Arena of Solution' leads a deliverance and prophetic ministry with a following of 2.5 million people across the major social media platforms. His church broadcasts a weekly stream of live services where a mélange of miracles are performed with each week's event seemingly outdoing the last as subscriber figures mount. During one live service, several people had come forward to the stage for deliverance with each performing in states of euphoric bliss. Many were twitching, shrieking, and swinging their arms about, utterly oblivious to the world around them. The cameras soon centred on one young man struggling to contain a sizeable erection. Stagehands aimed a microphone at him to reveal a dirty-talking demon speaking from within him. Audiences soon learned that the man had been suffering agonising pain from his pounding erection for twenty days. Without flinching, the prophet instructed the man to unzip his jeans, revealing a six-inch erection bulging through his cotton boxer shorts. As the man writhed around on the floor in distress thrusting his hips, the prophet further complicated matters by pouring holy water on the troubling member, all the while praying to eject the demon. The camera cut to women in the audience, some stunned by the scene while others shed tears of compassion as they witnessed the miracle and prayed along. Several minutes passed yet the erection remained sustained, but the prophet declared the miracle complete, adding that by nightfall the man would experience relief. The man returned a few Sundays later to give a testimony confirming that the miracle indeed came to completion, as he was now free of the erection demon. He was presented with a cash prize of ₦930,000 (approx. £1,850) cheered on by the audience.[24] Some observers prematurely concluded that Prophet Jeremiah could never surpass that stunt. He shocked his critics by following up with an astonishing weight loss miracle where 'fat loss blocking' demons were banished. An obese immobile forty-stone woman was wheeled in for the miracle in which the prophet cast out the 'spirit of obesity' and she rose to her feet to walk despite failing to stand in

[24] Christ Mercyland YouTube channel. (2017) *Prophet Jeremiah casts out erection demon.* YouTube.com

the preceding two years. The congregation erupted in ecstatic singing and dance.

Rather than pray against 'husband blocking demons' supposedly plaguing single women as other preachers do, Jeremiah simply asks singletons from within the congregation to line up on stage in pairs and weds them in instant marriage miracles, banishing the dreaded 'curse of the spinster.'

During one deliverance service for children, Jeremiah's televised event featured lengthy exorcism segments in which children were set free of demons and evil spirits. Performances included a boy who had been possessed by the spirit of a lion and a young girl consumed by a shapeshifting mermaid-serpent demon, which was seemingly triggered by secular music causing her to dance seductively against her will in front of an audience of adults. For the special service, the usually carpeted church stage had been replaced with an enormous sandpit allowing the children room to perform impressive gymnastic stunts as they reacted to the prophet's anointed handkerchief which unseen to the naked eye, supposedly appeared to demons as a scorching ball of fire.

With newcomers to the pulpit having to follow such extraordinary acts, churchgoers can expect more than conventional miracles of eyesight restoration or freedom from wheelchairs with the guarantee of experiences that supersede any comparable equivalent on TV or film with the added bonus of participation. Immersive miracle experiences often include catchall blessings such as deliverance from demons that cause procrastination, laziness, stress, anxiety, or forgetfulness, for which the majority of audiences would benefit. Instant money miracles infinitely prove popular with audience members discovering foreign currency stashed in their pockets, handbags, headwraps, or tucked between their Bibles. However, the house ultimately wins, as the funds are recouped through offering, tithe, and thanksgiving collections.

Some recent Pentecostal viral video trends have included mass hypnosis sessions during services in which audience members perform to the whim of the preacher who demonstrates his supernatural prowess by reducing followers to zombies to the astonishment of new converts who eagerly part with their cash. After standard offerings and tithes have been collected, those anticipating exceptional favour in the form of a miracle are encouraged to sow 'seeds of faith' with cash down payments of specified amounts in a never-ending pact with God. Generations of families have been driven to bankruptcy after entering the spiritually bound money pacts.

Central to the Pentecostal experience is performance in a form that is loose, participatory, immersive and closer to traditional religious worship than the Christianity introduced by missionaries. It would seem that Nigerian Pentecostalism is now bigger than Jesus and salvation is merely a side attraction, (See fig. 3) as emphasis shifts to the experience of the individual.

Since religious expression manifests through resources of indigenous cultures, the Pentecostal movement placed strong emphasis on this aspect, with Africans appropriating its charismatic aspects from the time of their early contact with the gospel. The very process of creative appropriation of Christianity is an exercise in self-definition and autonomous expression. Martin (2002) notes that; "the dynamic of Pentecostal populism, and of its partial restriction within the religious sphere, includes the paradox that autonomy relies on dependence, as equality depends on differences of power, and participation on authority." As time goes by, converts break free from the established order to create and occupy their own space.

This shift echoes the many parallels to be drawn between Nollywood and the new Pentecostal movement where inherited European traditions are appropriated in indigenous forms. The first Nigerian feature film *Palaver* (1926) a propaganda piece of the 'civilising mission' trope was directed by a Brit, but the creatives of the video film era reappropriated the medium to produce content that actually reflected their society. Likewise, the key players of the early Pentecostal movement reimagined Christianity in native ways, which gave rise to the creation of a new wave of the doctrine in ways that are intrinsically local.

While the stage antics of modern megachurches may have been inspired by Nollywood, the church may have surpassed the industry in its ability to not only command and retain audiences but generate income.

CHAPTER 6

Religion and cultural production

A commonplace analysis of the rise of religious fundamentalism in Africa is the persistent narrative of deprivation, poverty and state failure as the key undercurrent factors in the proliferation of Islamist extremism and Pentecostalism. But beyond that, there are complex, sometimes paradoxical explanations for these shifts especially in Nigeria which stands alone as the only nation with an almost equal demographic split of Muslims and Christians. The explosion of Pentecostalism was in part is fuelled by threats from

Muslim military leaders to officiate Sharia Law in as many states as possible, with some quarters advocating for a unified Islamic republic. Decades on, unrelenting Christianity in turn seemingly agitated Muslim Fulani herdsmen in their drive to expand their territorial dominance, leaving as many as 6,000 Christians dead between 2015 and 2019. While the herdsmen waged domestic jihad through land grab, their paramilitary counterparts beheaded Christian hostages in gruesome ISIS-style videos. Religious strife in Nigeria is seemingly a never-ending struggle with youths at university campuses frequently engaged with contesting opposing beliefs. However, both groups share a common ground – the outright rejection of secularism, paganism and any practice that questions the authority of the Abrahamic God. Their commonalities are reinforced in almost every facet of public life with parallel attitudes to practices such as witchcraft and women's rights. This idiosyncrasy produced the phenomenon of 'Chrislam,' originating in the South West in the 1970s. Defying the conventional disparities and the geographical boundaries that had long separated both factions in the

Muslim north and the Christian south, their alliance is at odds with concurrent ethnic and religious strife that has raged in the region for centuries. Nigerian Chrislamist sects Ifeoluwa, Oke Tude and the Ogbomoso Society were led by Muslim-turned-Christians who sought to amalgamate both creeds and transcend red lines by drawing on their commonalities.

Islamic influence in shaping the story of Nigeria echoes narratives that mirror the complexities of colonial rule. While the British narrative of invasion as a benevolent civilising mission crumbled soon after implementation, Islamic imperialism is still largely attributed to a trade process sidestepping the violent obliteration of pre-Islamic culture. These events led to the understanding of northern identity as primarily religious rather than ethnic. Little is left of animist religion, culture and history in the north practised by a now almost-annihilated tribe of the *Maguzawa* which in Hausa loosely means 'refusers of Islam.' From its sword-wielding origins to current contemporary manifestations of guerrilla warfare, Islamist tendencies run deep in the national psyche and not only among Muslims. Despite its destructive nature in its extreme manifestation by militant groups such as Ansaru and Boko Haram, Islam has served to revitalise Nigerian cultural expression in pioneering ways evident in film, music and literature.

Islamic influence on music and literature

Islamist dominance in the north today can be traced to the Fulani Jihad of the early 19th century but southerners had coexisted with pacifist Muslims for at least two centuries before the insurgency of Usman dan Fodio. Yorubaland with strategic coastal outposts had long facilitated a culture of inter-ethnic and religious mixing (in as much as outsiders were willing to assimilate) thus enabling the settlement of Sufi Muslims from northern Africa who brought with them the practice of mysticism along with rituals such as Ramadan. Many were learned multilingual clerics who had undertaken the Hajj pilgrimage to Mecca. The wealth of the new migrants afforded them audiences with local chiefs and royalty who entertained their eccentricities. The practice of Ramadan which is centred on restraint from earthly pleasures was marked by fasting only to be broken by prayer and a meal at dawn. The Yoruba referred to the bewildering practices of their Muslim guests as *Esin Imale* (the religion of the Malians) and across the land, Ramadan became a communal fiesta celebrated with lavish feasts, music and dance.

As the migrant Muslim population among the Yoruba grew, the first mosque in the south was built in Oyo-Ile in 1550 (Gbadamosi, 1978). Malian mannerisms such as flamboyant dressing and their polygamous nature became social signifiers of wealth which many locals were keen to emulate. The tradition of musicians providing entertainment to the Malian Muslims lodged at royal courts evolved into the performance of *sari* music which developed into *wéré,* and decades later created commercialised offshoots of *jùjú, fuji, waka, sakara, sekere, apala* and other indigenous Yorùbá music styles. Ramadan festivities came to be celebrated by both Muslims and non-Muslims with emphasis on the shared feast, known in Yorùbá as *sari*. The music combined percussion and *oriki* (traditional praise poetry) serving to wake people up to eat *sari*. The performers of this rite were known as *ajisari*, which in

Yorùbá means to wake up for *sari*. In the early days, the *ajisari* pounded pavements and his drums purely as an altruistic endeavour, much like the solitary town-square evangelist. But as time went by, the practice became recognised as musicianship and bands of up to a dozen members began performing more complex compositions. Collectively known as *ajiwere* or *oniwere* (performer of *wéré*, a wakeup call) the stakes soon became higher with grand prizes presented to the most popular bands. With the success of *wéré* musicians such as Alhaji Dauda Epo-Akara and Alhaji Sikiru Ayinde Barrister who released more than seventy studio albums, by the early 1970s the reach of the music had expanded beyond its original function, now serving as all-purpose celebration music.

The Ramadan tradition in effect created an explosion of Islamic-inspired Yorùbá music that would go global as a key Nigerian export with the international success of 'world music' acts such as King Sunny Ade, Ebenezer Obey, King Wasiu Ayinde aka K1 De Ultimate, Rahimi Ayinde aka Bokote, Alhaji Ayinla Kollington, and his wife Queen Salawa Abeni, with some signing major deals with Island Records and

Sony Music and later undertaking European and North American tours.

Rather than take inspiration from Malian traditional music which is largely string-led, played on the kora with its composer playing meditatively while sitting, these forms of Yorùbá music were rooted in percussion, utilising an array of indigenous instruments. Performances are more spirited and require full-bodied engagement with the hands and feet to activate movement and rhythm. The most popular style - *fuji* was a far cry from Afrobeat, the protest music of Fela Kuti, for *fuji* – in a nod to its roots in *wéré,* was about celebration. The essence of the music and the sheer bliss it produces is best captured by the king of *jùjú* music Sunny Ade's sentiment, when he appointed himself the 'Minister of Enjoyment.' As part of the tradition, Yorùbá musicians have a tendency for self-aggrandisement evidenced by fancy titles and monikers, with the public often expecting them to declare their own brilliance before buying in. *Fuji* also connotes *faaji*, which in Yorùbá means pleasure although *fuji* was coined spontaneously by Barrister.

For more than hundred years, the town of Ijebu

Ode has hosted an annual festival *Ileya*, also referred to as the *Ojude Oba* (the king's court) customarily held on the third day of Eid al-Adha. The Yoruba-Islamic festival draws an average of one million people from around the country and beyond.

While Islamic tradition in this context had materialised productively, not only in the creation of new works but in facilitating the assimilation of Muslims in the south, a darker picture has emerged in recent times in which musicians have been sentenced to death for blasphemy against the Prophet Muhammad. The increasing culling of freedoms in Nigeria's northern states today presents a paradox seen in overarching gender inequity contrasted with the forms of creative expression it unwittingly produced. Sharia law is implemented in twelve states, some of which are known to represent some of the worst gender disparities in the world. The region and in effect the country is continually ranked as one of the most unfortunate places to be born female along with Afghanistan, Syria, Somalia and Yemen with little recourse to education, reproductive rights or sexual autonomy. Official sanctions enable sexual violence on an endemic scale, permissible through the morality police who are taxed to instil correction by abuse as well as lax child marriage laws that have wreaked havoc on young women's bodies, evidenced by health conditions such as obstetric fistula which incapacitates millions of teenage girls annually.

Like the subversive actions of Pentecostal women, which is explored in Chapter 8, the women and girls of northern Nigeria began producing expressive creative responses to the subjugating conditions they lived under. At the height of Boko Haram's insurgency, the capture of more than 200 girls from Chibok Secondary School in 2014 marked their most prolific raid to date. Some of the captives lost their lives trying to escape, some were forced into harems to birth the offspring of the fighters, some were compelled to become suicide bombers while others simply stayed out of exhaustion, unconvinced that they had a society worth returning to. One survivor – Patience Ibrahim's experience is documented in the harrowing book *A Gift from Darkness* (2017). The choice of literature as Ibrahim's cathartic mode of response in making sense of her ordeal continues a tradition of women's resistance to

Islamism in the north of Nigeria. In Hausa drama and oral tradition, *Littattafan Soyayya* (books of love) is romantic fiction written in the Hausa language by women for women, and has circulated since the 1980s at Kano markets. In the last decade, the genre has been repurposed by a new generation of writers who are often women and girls whose only experience of male-female relationships have been marred by violent encounters, and therefore turn to writing romance as a form of escapism. Girls in captivity may write on days they are deemed 'unclean' during their menstrual cycles, temporarily banished from the preying hands of their captors. Each copy of the pamphlets or zines are circulated in covert ways and its informal authoring and nondescript binding means the stories can be expanded upon by each new reader. The very act of women writing in a region under siege by tyrants who have declared that 'Western education is forbidden,' particularly to women, is a transgressive endeavour that drives home the notion of the medium as the message.

Nigerian Christian films

Actor, writer, director, producer and evangelist Mike Bamiloye's ministry is a key example of an establishment that sought to converge the power of film with the authority of the church to amass an audience. Established in 1985, Bamiloye's Mount Zion Drama Ministry has released more than fifty productions to date with films that centre on morality tales with a heavy focus on the last chapter of the Bible. Originating as a roving theatre company creating presentations for church stages, the troop ministered through drama performances, which were followed by alter calls for salvation. After years of delivering stage shows across Nigeria, Ghana, Cameroon and Kenya, the organisation expanded into a film production company with titles such as *Lost Forever* and *Ultimate Power (Ayamatanga)* relying heavily on the fire and brimstone warnings in the Book of Revelation. In each film, those who heed the salvation message are rewarded with a place in heaven, while the wicked unbelievers are accompanied by demons to the bottomless pit of hell where they perish eternally.

Mount Zion films utilised plotlines that placed special emphasis on punishment for Africans who rejected the message of Christ in favour of indigenous beliefs. In titles such as *Esin Ajoji (The Strange Religion)*, *The Gods are Dead* and *Apoti Eri (The Ark of God)* characters who performed rituals and participated in idol worship were compelled to either accept Jesus or be damned.

Bamiloye described his foray into film as a divine calling which functioned to create an alternative to secular movies.[25] As a scriptwriter and director, Bamiloye revealed his continual study of Nollywood to inform his process and aesthetic choices but taking inspiration from a higher power. The Mount Zion Institute of Christian Drama provides training through annual courses and boasts more than 1,200 graduates to date.

Produced in both English and Yorùbá with multi-language subtitles, Mount Zion films alongside other church-funded films created a robust subgenre of gospel-cum-horror titles that enjoyed wide broadcast on national television, across unaffiliated churches,

---

[25] The Daily Independent (2013) *How we moved from church drama to movies – Bamiloye.* Dailyindependentnig.com

schools, campus conventions and hospitals. For the latter institution, the films may have served to reduce their reliance on the rota of preachers seeking to convince those on their deathbed to accept Christ.

Whilst these gospel genre films carry a PG classification, they are often shown to young children and to date, they remain the most nightmare-inducing Nollywood films I have ever watched not only because they featured witches, demons and burning bodies but because almost every misdemeanour was punished fatally - from children who begged for snacks in the playground, to liars and cheats as well as all assortments of Jesus deniers including witches, mermaids, *Orisa* worshipers, Muslims, Satanists and atheists. Such characters would often meet a ghastlier end than even Judas Iscariot. Titles such as *Scores to Settle* (1998) starring A-list trio Liz Benson, Richard Mofe-Damijo and Omotola Jalade featured scenes in which married men who paid young women for sex were dismembered with unforgiving close-ups of their severed penises. *End of the Wicked* (1999) produced by notorious evangelist Helen Ukpabio and directed by Nollywood heavyweight Teco Benson features a graphic lesbian rape scene in which a possessed woman brandishes a large black dildo to carry out the attack on her daughter-in-law.

Ironically, rather than serve to deter children like me from committing sin, gospel films opened up various avenues of curiosity previously unknown to me. In their attempt to impart fundamentalist and behavioural moral codes on the young, Mount Zion film producers may have left many fragile minds scarred by the experience.

CHAPTER 7

Performative prayer

In the Christian Protestant tradition, Pentecostals are distinct from other holiness movements in their abidance to Holy Spirit baptism. This distinction is marked by the ability to speak in tongues (glossolalia) as well as other spiritual gifts such as prophecy and healing. A strand of Pentecostalism emerged in America in the early 20th century, pioneered by evangelist Charles Parham who alongside his protégé William Seymour were both crucial in underscoring and demonstrating that the linguistic ability to perform glossolalia was evidence for the baptism of the Holy Spirit. Parham who began conducting religious services without formal training since the age of fifteen had grown to increasing frustration with the hierarchical scholarly system of the Methodist church preferring to evangelise by direct inspiration. His ministry was a heavy influence on Seymour, an African-American preacher who convened the Azusa Street Revival, which is considered by many to as the birthplace of American Pentecostalism, which is a wholly different phenomenon to Nigerian Pentecostalism, which has its native roots in the *Aladura* movement originating in Ijebu-Ode in 1918.

The significance of the Pentecost, also known as the Feast of Weeks is described in the Book of Acts commemorating the descent of the Holy Spirit on the disciples and followers of Jesus as they gathered in Jerusalem. Together they experienced a divine visitation described as a 'mighty rushing wind', evidencing the presence of the Holy Spirit due to the 'tongues of fire' in which they began to speak. Each of those present; the twelve Apostles, Jesus' brothers, his mother Mary more than a hundred other followers each spoke in a different tongue. For Christians, this event marked the fulfilment of the prophecy of Joel that Christ will baptise his followers in the spirit. Parham and Seymour were instrumental in re-awakening the Holy Spirit fire among modern-day Christians, with their radical non-racially segregated events sending shockwaves across America.

The performance of glossolalia - speaking in tongues using improvisation techniques that string together what are essentially nonsense syllables extends to creative performative contexts outside the church particularly in vocal music. These are evident in examples such as scat singing in bebop-era jazz elevated to high art by Ella Fitzgerald, indigenous practices of lilting (mouth music) in Gaelic-speaking regions, drum-led West African music - a form of verbal art, and in contemporary hip-hop by artists such as Eazy-E in *Eazy Street* (1990). Adriano Celentano's 1972 song *Prisencolinensinainciusol* completely relies on uttering gibberish in an upbeat American accent, an experiment described by the musician as "a new language that no one will understand." Indeed, the song is popular for representing what English sounds like to non-speakers yet failing to make any sense to natives. Some Pentecostals argue that while glossolalia may sound unintelligible to laymen, the entity to whom the prayers are said fully comprehends it. For participants, there is a sense of euphoria to be enjoyed from the collective exercise and the freedom to use one's voice for spontaneous outbursts that are rewarded positively. It is not unusual to witness tongues-of-fire rap battles on stage at youth churches or find YouTube tutorials on learning glossolalia techniques. It is increasingly recognised as a form of performative expression that once finessed, can be repurposed to engage, dazzle and entertain the public.

From my recollection during many hours spent at all-night prayer vigils as a child, performative styles of glossolalia adopted by each speaker tend not to be original formulations for each event. Instead, prayers follow a rhythm of a series of syllables which are uttered repetitively. Then after some time, a unique script is established and simply recited when needed. While I struggled to receive or demonstrate this supernatural gift, I was able to recognise and copy each of my parents' style and rhythm with ease. This impulse of flow demonstrated by praying people seemingly echoes vocal music traditions - Jazz legends Betty Carter and Sarah Vaughn both had distinctive go-to scatting styles that shared similarities in purpose, flow and delivery, yet unique to each.

Prayer in everyday life

Moving beyond the use of prayer as supplication and intercession, Pentecostals employ praise worship as both a form of thanksgiving and as a means of releasing emotional pain. Beyond praying for others, asking for favours or offering gratitude, prayer is also used to tackle battles within the self and against the enemy. For non-Pentecostal Christians, the intensity of a routine ritual like saying grace at mealtimes is a casual tone that generally applies to all other prayers. Whereas for Pentecostals, prayer is an incredibly bodily experience often described as spiritual warfare. (See fig. 8) In life, believers are often told to respond to transgressors through forgiveness and turning the other cheek. Therefore, it is only on the battlefield of prayer that they have the chance to fight back. Like a general commanding an army, prayer leaders embolden fellow soldiers of Christ with words of reinforcement before they make the collective charge towards the enemy. Prophesies, promises and miracles that were made in the Bible become flashpoints for action. The congregation is reminded of the never-ending war that must be fought against Satan until the Last Day with frequent warnings that anyone who fails to pray becomes the enemies' prey. Events designed to train converts from mere followers into prayer warriors range from hour-long intercessions to all-night vigils, up to the gold standard of forty-days and forty-nights of prayer and fasting, which echo durational performances by body-focused endurance artists such as Marina Abramović, Chris Burden and Tehching Hsieh.

Like the performance of miracles by churchgoers to signal their status as worthy of healing, the ability to pray like a warrior is another signifier of spiritual status within the church hierarchy. Not only does it present the performer as possessing clarity on ambiguous matters of spirituality, but it also affirms they have authority over evil forces and most importantly, it confirms their piety, evidenced by Holy Spirit baptism.

The ripples of prayer performance have spread so far beyond the church into Nigerian society such that the public is not always able to opt-out. Willingness to pray or the ability to demonstrate proficiency at praying can at times, be used to suggest one's innocence or establish authority since the (most convincing) performer is deemed closer to God. For example, it is commonplace for collective prayers to be said before interstate travel on public transport, such that any passenger unwilling to participate is viewed with suspicion. Should an accident occur en route, the prayer refusenik is believed to be complicit and can be held accountable.

CHAPTER 8

Pentecostals, gender, and sexuality

In contemporary contexts, few Christians interpret or apply the gospels literally but nonetheless, a precedent and history of women's subjugation in the church remain evident. Apostle Paul's mandate required women to remain silent in church and submit, leaving questions to their husbands to avoid bringing 'disgrace'. Today, Pentecostal women professing charismatic gifts are commonplace in contrast with older European churches, some of which barred women from ministerial duties and public worship.

In indigenous worship settings, women have been prominent – from temple priestesses to diviners and herbalists, the image of women as healers is inherent in the African worldview. Nigerian Pentecostalism has not only accommodated women in its ranks but has placed them at its core. Although rather than achieving gender equality brought on by increased democratisation, the position of women has been elevated within their communities by virtue of their leadership roles in the church. Mercy Oduyoye (1986) argues that patriarchy in African Christianity owes more to its borrowed practices from European liturgy than African tradition. Female ministers such as Helen Ukpabio who specialise in healing and deliverance ministries wield immense power since they reprise roles played by women in traditional African religions, offering gender-specific pastoral care and female solidarity among followers.

However, increased female leadership in itself does not necessarily allude to progression. Ukpabio, the founder of the Liberty Gospel Church, is a self-proclaimed witch-hunter and was the subject of a 2008 documentary on anti-witchcraft child abuse broadcast on Britain's Channel 4. The film prompted an outcry from the public, who successfully petitioned to curtail Ukpabio's ministerial visa to the UK on child protection grounds. In 2014 Ukpabio brought a libel case against her critics, suing the British Humanists Association for a mammoth sum of £500,000,000.

In male-founded churches, the pastor's wife often takes on a highly visible public role serving as a "nodal power point for mobilizing and deploying female evangelical power," as Kalu (2008) notes. As first ladies, they're externally visible in the posters and billboards promoting the church (See fig. 13). Kalu also suggests that pastors have opened the space for women for pragmatic purposes since wives are needed to co-pastor the church to ensure that all managerial and financial aspects remain confidential.

Given its once tight grip on women's reproductive rights, Western feminists have typically been critical of religion considering it "the major cultural reinforcer of modern industrial patriarchy" (Briggs, 1987). For them, the Christian faith for too long was an obstacle to emancipation but in the same regard, women of faith do not look to feminism for empowerment. With religiosity on the rise among Africans, the Western secular position is deemed unattractive, since African women for the most part do not subscribe to radical feminism.

Kalu notes that African women "do not reject the church, yearn for a women's church, or call for an exit from male-dominated churches… most remain loyalists." Kalu's loyalists are split into two categories: survivalists and elevationists. The former makes use of the church environment as a tool for survival to bolster the socioeconomic and emotional pressures they face in everyday life. While the elevationists may also be survivalist, they primarily use the church's resources to improve their own lives. Kalu argues that "This spirituality empowers women's capacity to confront society and to use the literacy and other skills that are nurtured within the church as tools in their daily lives and professions."

Feminist scholars Line Nyhagen and Beatrice Halsaa (2016) conducted an extensive study on religious women from migrant communities living in Norway, Spain and the UK delving into their views on citizenship, gender, feminism and religion. They reported that the women recognised the importance of feminism in the past and some of its positive impacts on the opening up of their religion but rejected feminism as 'extreme' and at odds with their own ethics and values. On the question of autonomy, Nyhagen and Halsaa argued its relativity, stating that "the changing panorama of political, economic, social, demographic, educational and cultural realities in which people live out their lives must be considered." The question of why women are often drawn to religious traditions that subordinate them still looms but Nyhagen and Halsaa frame the women's experiences in the West as largely marginalised and that the women were engaged in a "struggle against increasing global social inequalities and persisting gender inequalities." For them, the women's actions in their communities through organising, participation, and negotiation of citizenship and gender relations challenge the secularist notion of religion as a private matter since it would "produce social and political exclusion, non-recognition and a serious democratic conflict." While Nyhagen and Halsaa's approach provides some clearer gendered insights, the women's lived experiences cannot be framed as entirely independent of the workings of wider religious institutions. Their view also echoes the arguments of liberation theology which does not correlate with the experience of African Pentecostals who despite their otherness on foreign soil cannot be neatly categorised as merely an oppressed class.

A review of the role of women in the Pentecostal church again demonstrates the potential for enormous contradictions between ascribed and actual roles, and that contemporary critiques of church doctrines have given way to more nuanced interpretations of charismatic performance tropes to reveal powerful female archetypes. This is not to overlook how the lack of accountability can lead to the reinforcement of some of the darkest forms of gendered violence and patriarchy including sexual assault and child abuse within the church. Bishop David Oyedepo of Winners Chapel brazenly assaulted a child on stage during a 2009 deliverance service in a bid to "slap the witch out of her". Oyedepo, whose personal wealth was estimated by Forbes at $150 million, was later sued by activists for ₦2 billion ($5 million) for the 'slapsgiving' incident but the case was outrightly dismissed by a judge. Rather than cower under the pressure of international outrage, Oyedepo doubled down and insisted that far from seeking redress, the girl returned to appease him.[26]

Oyedepo may have been successful in squashing the assault charges against him but the evidence remains online for posterity. Rather than lobby for prosecution in cases of exploitation, abuse and assault, perhaps the downfall of corrupt leaders will lie in their own doing. As live-streaming and video services become the norm, more so in the post-pandemic age, church protocols are exposed to audiences beyond its immediate intended reach. The archival nature of the format means little can be withdrawn after its release into the public domain, leaving mega-preachers open to critical audiences who can review hours of footage, identify reappearing miracle performers and expose other inconsistencies. Likewise, the active social media presence of Pentecostal leaders leaves them vulnerable to impersonation, creating room for outlandish miracle

---

[26] Digital Journal. Didymus, J. (2011) *Bishop Oyedepo boasts about slapping teenage girl.* Digitaljournal.com

claims to be parodied, blurring the lines between what they purport is 'real' and what is fabricated by pranksters. In 2016, TB Joshua swiftly deleted his Facebook post prophesying Hillary Clinton's US presidential election win but in doing so, the prophet unwittingly garnered headlines and derision for his so-called prophetic gifts.

Pentecostalism and homosexuality

The presence of gay people in the Pentecostal church presents a challenge that has become increasingly difficult to dismiss. Their existence challenges a cornerstone of the church, posing a threat to the marriage institution which essentially functions to propagate the religion intergenerationally through reproduction. In a time of superfluous digital activism in relation to every imaginable cause, the church has been challenged to articulate its position on same-sex rights. Even in the European context, some Church of England bishops continue to oppose the ordination of gay clerics,[27] and expectedly their conservative stance has been met with strong criticism. Politicians such as former Liberal Democrat leader Tim Farron have faced scrutiny for their private views on homosexuality. In 2017 Farron was forced to declare that leading a progressive liberal party and being a committed Christian had at times felt "impossible."[28]

Pentecostals in the West have had to contend with shifts in the social landscape around them but rather than become engulfed in collective battles against marginalisation, they selectively identify with the left on single issues such as race and migration but demonstrate a closer alignment to the conservative right on social issues such as sexual and gender politics. Anderson (2004) noted; "Pentecostalism has in so many cases changed from being an apolitical and otherworldly movement to become a supporter of reactionary politics, not only in the USA, but in countries like Guatemala, Chile and South Africa... Pentecostals generally agree with the conservative

---

[27] The Guardian. Sherwood, H. (2017). *C of E bishops refuse to change stance on gay marriage.* Theguardian.com

[28] BBC News (2017). *Farron quits as Lib Dem leader over clash between faith and politics* Bbc.co.uk

Christian opposition to homosexual practice." In the Nigerian context, governments not only looked to churches to help validate their anti-gay policies, but Presidential candidates openly sought the approval of megachurch leaders such as in the case of Goodluck Jonathan and RCCG leader Enoch Adeboye in 2012.

Johnson (2008) examines the case of 'church sissies' and 'gayness in the black church' revealing the Pentecostal paradox around homosexuality in a region known for its fundamental religiosity, particularly among blacks, arguing that "despite the homophobia, both implicit and explicit, gay men are integral to most black church organisations." Johnson notes that the lifestyle practice of religion and adherence to institutional guidelines among blacks has always been nuanced, adding that "its progressive public face has often camouflaged more problematic internal policies and attitudes - sexism and homophobia being just two." With an emphasis on the stereotypical queer choir director, pianist or soloist often found in black churches, Johnson's interviews with black gay churchgoers suggested their presence is complex and often contradictory, referring to the church as "a place of comfort - a place where [ironically] they are first accepted, where they first felt a sense of community and belonging. Ultimately, it is a contradictory space, one that exploits the creative talents of its gay members even as it condemns their gayness, while also providing a nurturing space to hone those same talents." With music being a high value component of the Pentecostal experience, gay entertainers and queer presence remain integral to the institution and new fellowships are being created around them with a growing number of LGBT-friendly Pentecostal churches such as the House of Rainbow church in London led by an openly gay Nigerian minister. As one of Johnson's interviewees put it; "where else but in the black church can a queen be a star whether he has talent or not? Homophobic or not, church folk will give you your props." Gay Pentecostals present a contradictory rationale for remaining in the church, as on the one hand they acknowledge experiencing homophobia but on the other, they consider it a form of institutional discrimination that has no bearing on their personal relationship with God.

But while Pentecostal audiences seemingly overlook homosexuality, their acceptance of gay men is often limited to non-leadership roles. Some accept the conditions as part of a journey of progression to full integration, in a process that can be likened to minstrelsy. Minstrel shows originally designed to lampoon black people relegated black performers to playing denigrating roles, but it served ironically as the platform with which they made a name for themselves in the film industry before moving onto mainstream roles.

It is apparent that gay Pentecostals, particularly musicians are integral to the church but rather than the church being radically transformed by their presence, the institution is simply being preserved. Like the women worshippers, gay men subvert the limitations of Pentecostal conventions by embodying the space. Cartier (2013) drew on ideas of embodiment and experience which inform how spaces become places, observing how pre-Stonewall women's presence transformed gay bars to create space for themselves by embodying it, identifying the markers for such transformation as evidence for "community, affirmation of the sacredness of a people, and human capacity for transcendence."

CHAPTER 9

Black bodies in performance

The performance of fervent prayer and ecstatic worship have been contextualised as art forms in their own right, likened to the work of an actor in interpreting a play or script. For liturgy scholar Rabbi Lawrence Hoffman, the manifestation of prayer through chants and song to express individual thought and desire underscores the medium as a form of artistic expression.[29] In the Pentecostal context, self-styled

---

[29] The Times of Israel. Hoffman, L. (2013) *Prayer as Performance Art.*

prayer warriors take pride in building their stamina, displaying creativity in formulating prayers and speaking in tongues, akin to lyrical freestyling not unlike the intensity of the theatre stage.

In the same way that performance art is often defined by its affront to the establishment, zealous worship and all forms of 'worshiptainment' are also shunned in the broader Christian movement and is denounced by many as heresy,[30] perceived as a theatrical perversion of Christianity.

Prior to the flourishing movement of happenings and performance art in the 1960s, black performance had largely been contextualised as an extension of theatre rather than their understanding as art forms. The Black Arts Movement that evolved after the civil rights era not only harked back to the Harlem Renaissance of the 1920s but produced distinctive literary, musical and visual languages of which spirituality was often a feature. Hundred years on, African-American women churchgoers continue to

---

Jewishweek.timesofisrael.com

[30] Baptist News. Livingstone, M. (2014). *The Heresy of Worshiptainment*. Baptistnews.com

don extravagant hats that first originated during the renaissance and today Afro-Pentecostal women in other parts of the world continue to borrow from the tradition of wearing heaven-reaching hats thought to 'catch God's eye.'

Within the rebellious artistic outpouring of avant-garde expression, performance often functioned to reflect on the familiar, described by Oliver (2013) as the "theatre of the everyday and the ordinary". Performance, action and movement are so deeply entwined and difficult to distinguish. Examining the characteristics that define performance such as eccentricity, protest, endurance, confrontation, antagonism, combined with references to a historical linage and its roots in spectacle, radical black performance can be located and brought into the Pentecostal context. Racialised performance has often borrowed from traditions of black cultural expression that were not necessarily regarded as art. Oliver considered black performance as present in everyday life, and also as a "dysfunctional inheritance born from mastering both personal and communal survival", thus applicable to the struggle of gay Pentecostals, utilising their ability to entertain and perform as a means of earning their place and ensuring their continued survival within the institution.

In artworks such as *Diary of a Victorian Dandy* (1998), British-Nigerian artist Yinka Shonibare uses dandyism and self-imagery to offer a provocative response to the stereotypical representation of black men, recalling the flamboyance of the Sunday dress. For Ekow Eshun, curator of *Made You Look: Dandyism and Black Masculinity*, flamboyant dressing is used as a subversive tool to reveal maleness through performance. "For black men, the donning of stylish clothes acts as a form of radical personal politics, a deliberate transgression of social order that would otherwise render them unseen or beneath regard."[31]

In *Radical Presence: Black Performance in Contemporary Art* (Oliver, 2013) examines performance art as practised by black artists who have offered profound contributions to the genre. At times their work is considered radical solely by virtue of their skin colour

---

[31] Victoria and Albert Museum (2015) *"Staying Power – Photographs of Black British experience. Vam.ac.uk.*

given the context and placement of their interventions. Some have challenged and contested traditional performance art genres and the limitation of the formal white cube, pushing their work beyond the gallery context onto the streets to engage socially with the public. The characteristics of race and gender which previously meant the exclusion of those artists, was to later become their currency. *Radical Presence* argues that rather than define blackness or black performance, emphasis should be placed on acknowledging its existence, which only comes to being through experience.

Black performance artists who draw on the notion of the body as material often reach deep into historical narratives to reflect on contemporary struggles. As artists draw on the body as a material for the embodiment of suffering, it becomes a site of self-determination and liberation through performance.

There is vast potential for increased visibility of Pentecostal performance in art practice as evidenced in the work of artists who have staged happenings, actions, interventions and performances that borrow from religious ritual practices delivered with what can be deemed Pentecostal charisma.

Lorraine O'Grady staged guerrilla actions under the persona of *Mlle Bourgeoise Noire* (1980-1983) to critique prevalent racial apartheid in the art world at the time. Dressed as a fiery beauty queen, O'Grady crashed gallery openings as *MBN* and delivered a seething rebuke to hosts and audiences and her protests soon became recognised as performances in their own right. If the intent of her work was to change the art world, O'Grady considered her performances as ancillary to the intervention of Adrian Piper in earlier years. Piper's *Mythic Being* (1972-1981) was produced to instigate confrontational public encounters around race, gender and class. Aesthetically, the actions mirrored lonesome but charged monologues delivered by street preachers.

American sculptor Houston Conwill's *Juju Rituals* (1975-1983) drew on the aesthetics and philosophy of traditional African religion. As a former student of theology, Conwill's work blurred the boundaries between spiritual practice and performance, borne out of a desire to reflect on both history and myth that have 'travelled across continents and generations.' A critic described the strength of Conwill's work as its ability to "combine emotion and politics... in the creation of works that reframe African-American identity."[32]

Working in the vein of visceral spectacle, Ron Athey's work fuses Christian symbolism and rituals to create audacious performances inspired by his upbringing among a family of white evangelicals. Having gone public with his HIV-positive status, Athey shocked spectators with a participatory performance in 1994 that called for audience contact with (what was presumed to be his) blood evoking the flesh and blood covenant of the Last Supper. Athey soon found himself blacklisted from the art scene but in recent times, his work has found a new following among a young generation of Americans who seek meaning and purpose in a post-secular world.

In the spirit of these artistic works and creative practices, can the Pentecostal stage function as a site for radical black expression? Beyond the blasphemous trope – such as Andres Serrano's *Piss Christ* (1987) a crucifix submerged in the artist's urine, and John

---

[32] The New York Times. Roberts, S. (2016) *Houston Conwill, Whose Sculptures Celebrated Black Culture, Dies at 69* Nytimes.com

Latham's *God is Great* (1991) desecrating the Bible, the Quran and the Torah, artists often borrow from charismatic religious practices to perform interventions. In another intervention, members of the Blue Rider Collective were arrested for 'performing an exorcism' on Lenin's body in Moscow's Red Square by dousing the mausoleum in holy water. [33]

Others such as Peter de Cupere, have relied on Christian aesthetics to question positions occupied by women. In *Deflowering* (2014) Cupere collects the water from an ice Madonna sculpture placed on a woman's vagina to produce melting holy water. Audiences were invited to touch the sacred water to "explore the space between the divine and embodied representations of women." [34]

Performance art often transcends its primary setting, spilling into political activism to reach audiences beyond the gallery space. Can performativity in the church also transcend its immediate setting and

[33] Artnet News. Neuendorf, H. (2015). *Russian Performance Artists Arrested for Exorcizing Lenin* Artnet.com

[34] The Huffington Post. Frank, P. (2014) *Olfactory Artist Has Crafted A Sculpture That Smells Like Vagina.* Huffingtonpost.com

become absorbed into broader discourses of black radical expression? In the confessional age of social media, a growing pool of consumers are prone to participate only in offline events that promise increased online visibility. For some, evidential engagement with spirituality is a good enough reason to participate, encouraged by the allure of a waiting virtual stage to express exhibitionist tendencies, although the benefits also extend to non-exhibitionists. Cox (2001) argued for charismatic expression as a form of empowerment in modern society, due to an 'ecstasy deficit' allowing such spiritual experiences to enable people to gain deeper awareness. With Pentecostals often withdrawing from social activities, the church stage serves as a platform for expression and an avenue for releasing angst, with the promise of transformative experiences in unexpected ways.

Aesthetically, there are parallels to be drawn between performances by black artists operating within galleries and public spaces and the ecstatic worship of Afro-Pentecostals. As part of a radical tradition originating within the civil rights movement, black aesthetics emphasise cultural production for and by black people. In *Diary of a Victorian Dandy* (1998), Yinka Shonibare uses dandyism and self-imagery to offer a provocative response to the constrained stereotypical representation of black men. Ike Ude's post-dandyism portrait series *Sartorial Anarchy* explores duality within identities that are otherwise inhibited. Echoing artists such as Shonibare and Ude whose works heavily utilise black aesthetics to reimagine the world, gay Pentecostal choristers can be said to attempt to disrupt the social order by creating transgressive hyper-visible representations of themselves. Performative actions such as the ecstatic deliverance rituals led by women reveal an undercurrent of subversion of the status quo, mirroring a factor that has always been integral to the rise of Pentecostalism.

Coleman (2008) in *Womanist Theology* suggests that minorities and queers represent the burdened figure of Christ. "Postmodernist womanist theology argues that a black woman is often Christ. The saviour may be a teenager, a person living with a disability, or a lesbian woman." Charismatic expression comes to play a dual role within the church since the success of Pentecostalism relies on theatrics. Entertainment provided by minorities is key to ensuring its expansion and cultural relevance, yet it is also the medium utilised by performers to subvert the established conventions and limitations imposed by authorities – allowing them to experience momentary bouts of freedom unafforded elsewhere.

Kanye West and the Sunday Service Choir

Kanye West's *Sunday Service* (2019-) epitomises the Pentecostal tendency to present worship as spectacle. As an ensemble, it is comprised of 166 musicians who have performed hour-long weekly concerts at venues ranging from prisons to music festivals, concert arenas, and Paris Fashion Week to Joel Osteen's Lakewood church – a megachurch with one of the largest congregations in America. With a highly stylised aesthetic, West's choir members appear in exclusive *Yeezy*-designed outfits and assume formative structures not unlike his fashion shows. *Sunday Service* is purposefully Instagram-friendly and is attended by a roll call of celebrities and entertainers for clout. Attendees such as David Letterman have attested that he found the encounter to be "moving and inspirational" and "better experienced than described." With sets that rouse audiences by fusing gospel-inspired remixes with original numbers, fashion and music magazine columnists waxed lyrical about the innovative aspects of West's latest offerings, but commentators from the corners of Black Twitter appeared baffled, claiming the gospel mashups and performances were simply routine at black churches on any given Sunday.

Known to flirt with both the radical left and the alt-right, West who declared himself 'Yeezus', has in the past donned Confederate iconography as fashion, and in 2018 heaped praise on President Trump, who is considered by many as an antithesis to everything progressive - a man seemingly beyond redemption. Many observers have read West's actions in a literal sense often misunderstanding the symbolic context of the gesture that saw a postmodern messiah offer an olive branch to a man almost unanimously condemned by the world. Distinctly fearless and unafraid to rock the boat, West's oeuvre is subversion, and his antics make him arguably hip-hop's last renegade.

CHAPTER 10

Going global: the reverse mission

As the independence movement peaked in Africa with seventeen nations regaining their leadership from colonisers in 1960, it was commonly thought that Christianity would plummet into rapid decline. Developments in the following decades not only falsified this prediction but produced an unexpected outcome where Africans began taking Christianity back to the West in a phenomenon known as the reverse mission. African Pentecostals often perceive the gospel as a seed that was planted by European missionaries, and having bloomed, they seek to return it to its roots, a task of increasing importance for the African diaspora in the face of Christianity's global decline. If the aim of the reverse missionaries is to transform the new world they inhabit, the key to expansion lies in strategies that solidify their social, cultural and political relevance. As such their operative mode calls for the implementation of the social gospel, in which the church exerts its influence in shaping the community around it. For example, the UK's Harbour Church outlines its mission as 'evangelising the nation and transforming society.' The evangelical's self-assigned mandate to change the world is often accompanied with urgency, linked to the doctrine of the End Times, with a belief that there is a golden window within which to usher in change. The Pentecostal social strategy has been replicated among many churches who carry out crucial social functions that fall short of state provision.

Under Tony Blair's premiership, the Labour Party implemented a number of multicultural policies that relied on community leaders to represent the interests of minority groups. Many of these roles were occupied by religious organisations sometimes to the detriment of the cause, as some parts of society became more fragmented. However, some churches were able to seize the opportunity to intervene on escalating knife crime which reached endemic levels among black male youths. By operating as mediators between young people and law enforcement, churches staged services, discussions, workshops, street and online outreach programmes to tackle gang violence in inner London boroughs. At churches such as SPAC Nation in South London, assault weapons, knives, guns and drugs are routinely given up during alter calls by balaclava-wearing gang members. SPAC was founded by Nigerian-born Tobi Adeboyega whose ministry engages with otherwise hard to reach young men providing entrepreneurship training alongside spiritual mentoring. The transformative work of the church in youth crime intervention has produced a long list of former gang-members-turned-preachers such as Kevin Yfeko, Enrique Uwadiae and Mo Timbo.

The expansion and activities of House on the Rock demonstrates the reverse mission and the social gospel strategy in action. With a significant presence in both

Nigeria and the UK, its headquarters the Rock Cathedral in Lagos - as well as being a place of worship, is branded as a centre for social justice to 'serve God in the community.' The grounds accommodate a 10,000-capacity auditorium, a hospital, a primary and secondary school, a theology college, and a drug rehabilitation clinic. In London, its Rock Tower in Tufnell Park is home to a youth club, hosts music, theatre and film productions, talent nights and runs a food bank with services open to the public.

Wilkinson's (2012) collection of essays explores global Pentecostal movements in the context of their public role, noting that its "transcendent aspects such as healing, combined with the internal (its leadership and organisation) as well as the external (its social and transnational networks), help shape civic engagement."

As Pentecostalism spread to Europe it successfully lent itself to adapting to new environments without diluting its native core characteristics. The growing traction abroad in new host communities proves it is not restricted by a fixed geographical centre. For example, the Embassy of the Blessed Kingdom of God for All Nations, with 50,000 followers in Kiev,

Ukraine, is pastored by Nigerian-born Sunday Adelaja and is considered Europe's third-largest church. Pentecostal churches across Europe often make robust charitable contributions to the homelands of their members. They are involved in addressing health crisis, hospital building, establishing schools and universities, expanding their role far beyond its religious scope. The phenomenon of African-founded churches in Europe reaching back to their African homelands has resulted in what some observers have deemed a "double reverse mission."[35]

Despite the gradual decline in religiosity among Britons, black majority churches (BMCs), continue to command a growing audience. While attendance has dwindled in the Church of England,[36] the reverse has occurred in BMCs which are reinvigorating Pentecostalism, representing the fastest growing form of Christianity in the world. A 2016 study found that for every 1.5-mile walk in Southwark, there were approximately twenty-five BMCs, totalling 240 in the

---

[35] Pew Trusts (2016). *How Africa Is Changing Faith Around the World*. Trend.pewtrusts.org
[36] The Telegraph. Bingham, J. (2016) *Church of England attendance plunges to record low* Telegraph.co.uk

borough.[37] Another study showed that for every person leaving the mainstream (white) church, as many are joining the black church.[38] This emergent demographic, largely comprised of newly emigrated Africans are often faced with embracing new forms of identity in a plural society where their tribal identity no longer holds the same importance. Where first-generation American Pentecostals at the Azusa Street Revival in 1906 may have argued that the church functioned as a racial leveller in bringing whites and blacks together, their contemporary counterparts may see their religious identity as a marker of otherness. As new migrants to Britain still finding their feet, they might be confined to low wage employment saddled with high living costs, compelling them to forge solidarity mechanisms. As such, they might find themselves pushed to the fringes of the cities, inhabiting the least desirable neighbourhoods in which

---

[37] Rogers, A. (2016) *How are black majority churches growing in the UK? A London Borough case study*. Religion and the Public Sphere. Blogs.lse.ac.uk

[38] Brierley (2006) reported that between 1998 and 2005, non-white church attendance in England increased by 19%, while white church attendance decreased by 19%. Growth in attendance comes primarily from Pentecostal churches: Brierley notes that these churches showed a 30% increase between 2005 and 2012, accounting for just over half (52%) of all churchgoers in London.

social service provisions are overstretched. Therefore, their coming together to worship is not only for belief but as a strategy for survival. As they strive to solidify their residency status, their reliance on their spiritual network is magnified in light of the threat of tighter migration policies. In many London churches, such as the Mountain of Fire Ministries, it is not unusual for Sunday services and prayer vigils to be entirely dedicated to themes of migration, featuring testimonials of 'divine intervention' on legal cases, 'spiritual breakthroughs' on appeals or deportation orders and fervent prayer and fasting for resident permits. Establishing strong religious identities therefore becomes a source of sustenance for migrants.

Pentecostal churches in the UK often attract African nationals from different parts of the continent. Many may have experienced racialisation and an awareness of their collective identity as 'black' for the first time following their arrival in Europe. Ethnic and tribal differences which are heightened on the continent take a secondary role, as members come to share a unifying (spiritual) language helping to foster democratic values such as tolerance, respect, and compromise. In this regard, the church is seen to provide security in times of uncertainty, reinforce identity, and empower its followers bridging the gap between them and the society, where everything is not only foreign but is of the (unbelieving) world.

For some members, the criteria for finding a new church to call their spiritual home rests on its capacity to deliver the security they need, with many migrants re-learning the concept of citizenship through the church. Particularly in the UK, where many churches hold charitable status and openly strive to provide social services, the church helps the new immigrant navigate the challenges of raising a family in western culture and in turn, it can expect to earn the long-term membership of their offspring.

Kalu (2008) warns that it would be a mistake to interpret the movement as a form of 'cultural nationalism,' as Pentecostals do not embrace the anti-western sentiment often prevalent among new converts within other religious sects such as Islam. Unlike Muslim converts or isolated Christian factions such as Jehovah's Witnesses, Pentecostals rarely withdraw from society - rather they long to be recognised by the world for their accomplishments. While Islam in its fundamentalist forms relies on strategies that destabilise the political order to force implementation of Sharia, Christian fundamentalists lobby the status quo. It is in their interest to comply with the State and gain influence over law-making processes. Therefore, the growing conversion rate in the Pentecostal movement is not perceived as a threat in the West to the same extent that scrutiny has been placed on other religious movements.

With the impact of globalisation, the function of religion in civic society becomes increasingly expanded and shaped by social forces. In the UK, the combination of austerity and the 'big society' discourse since the 2008 financial crash has led to increased democratisation of social service provision, enabling faith groups to take on more significant public roles to meet welfare needs. The developments call for a re-negotiation of societal organisation with an awareness of an apparent pushback against secularisation, forging the way for a return of religion to the public sphere. *'God is Back'* is the claim made by Micklethwait and Wooldridge (2009), probing the accepted notion that modernism has led to a decline in faith, or for Ian Leigh and Rex Ahdar (2012), *How God Never Really Went Away*, challenging the secularisation thesis that has long held sway in the West since Nietzsche announced the death of God. Their assertions are seemingly evidenced by increasing fundamentalism witnessed in different parts of the world – from the rise of Islamist jihadism across Africa to Hindu nationalism in India.

In 2014, the then Prime Minister David Cameron called for an expanded role for faith-based organisations in public life, underlining the re-emergence of the church as a social service provider. Cameron revealed that his 'big society' was a follow-on to Christ's leadership, but the announcement highlighted the increasing reliance of the State on other institutions to meet welfare needs. The unspoken undertone that accompanied the revelation was the need to reaffirm Britain as a Christian country in response to the growing contest among the major faith groups. While Cameron's sentiments were welcomed by Church of England bishops, secular institutions argued for religious neutrality in government, warning that special privileges for Christians would put social cohesion at risk.

Cameron had openly lobbied British-Nigerian voters at the RCCG's annual convention in 2015.[39] His successor Theresa May garnered criticism for the Conservative party's continued support of the church by LGBT critics who disapproved of the exorcisms performed there to turn gay people straight.[40] As the political capacity of the church expands, new challenges emerge, and concerns are raised about its treatment of its most marginalised members. As it assumes increased responsibility for welfare provision, questions arise regarding efficiency, as allocations are generally based on association rather than need.

Although the Pentecostal church provides a home and community for members, their business models create competition among pastors often leading to animosity, thus undermining the possibility of a cohesive movement for social change. New social divisions begin to emerge when those who are not 'born-again' are perceived as different, and inherently

[39] Quartz. Alake, O. (2015) *When UK PM Cameron attended a Nigerian church it showed the rise of the African vote.* Qz.com
[40] The Canary. Topple, S. (2017). *After Theresa May's visit to a homophobic church, the LGBTQ community turns and bites her on the arse.* Thecanary.co

excluded. Some churchgoers – although a marginal demographic, run the risk of being isolated from wider society due to limited engagement with others beyond their ethnoreligious communities. Many churches are set up to run events on numerous days of the week rotating between thanksgiving, deliverance, anointing, praise and worship services between Sunday services leaving members with little time for other activities. With growing memberships, church leaders have come to take on roles that are parallel to that occupied by politicians. Many UK megachurches have combined spiritual discipleship with life-skills training, community service, social activism and political engagement alongside theological teachings to enable their members to realise their aspirational goals. Formerly overlooked by the mainstream as a fringe movement of eccentric Africans, Afro-Pentecostals in Britain have long operated without accountability but as they seek increased visibility, they are compelled to make trade-offs. Preachers can expect demand for greater answerability than that required of their Africa-based counterparts since the public scrutiny often levied on politicians have become commonplace in the church, in some cases revealing allegations of fraud, money laundering, and convictions for sexual assault and child abuse.

Pentecostalism in its various forms over the last century is a global phenomenon manifesting locally with native inscriptions that reflect its dynamic expansive potential. Its explosion in Nigeria presents a compelling case for understanding the new modes of spirituality and emergent artistic forms within the movement. Nigerian Pentecostalism typifies another form of popular culture functioning as both a channel for spirituality and a form of immersive entertainment in which priority is placed on fulfilment of the self. Charismatic expression of faith, worship and fervent prayer exhibited through charged full-bodied performances override the traditional tenets laid out in the Bible. Emphasis is placed less on sacrificing worldly gains for assurance of paradise, and more on prosperity in the here and now. While some leaders have been guilty of exploitation, many have proved themselves as entrepreneurial by adapting creatively to the media-dominated world around them responding to audience demand as popular culture trends shift. Their ethics have often been reckless and unchecked, offering miracle healing, salvation, and eternal life, all for a price.

Nonetheless, Pentecostals should not be undermined as a sect only concerned with private morality, since Christianity itself has been reshaped and revived through the rise of Afro-Pentecostalism. The fervour they demonstrate for Christianity is strongly rooted in their desire to change the world around them, not unlike any other popular activist movement. However, the survival of Pentecostalism relies on its dynamism in responding to the changing social climate in places it sows new roots, as well as the developments emerging from within it particularly around gender and sexuality.

The role of Pentecostal women is not static and increasingly expands, with studies showing that their lived experiences are in opposition to commonly assumed perceptions. Not only are women the primary recruiters of new members to the church, but they are also responsible for its transformation into a cultural stage. With the success of female evangelical leaders and the prominence of the First Lady figure, the movement undeniably recognises the importance of women within it, unlike its unspoken reliance on queer musicians for entertainment. Rejecting much of the theology of conventional Christianity, Pentecostals define women's roles in a more egalitarian way. Symbolically, there are participatory opportunities opened up for them through performance, divination, and leadership of ecstatic spirit worship. Overall, they have much to gain through collective organising and peer support with access to opportunities that would otherwise be closed to them especially as first-generation migrant women.

Given that a mass exodus of Africans – particularly women from the church is a most unlikely event, societies that welcome migrant groups would fare better with a deeper understanding of the movement and the nuances that come with operating in the Pentecostal and secular world simultaneously - by establishing robust integration schemes.

While it is difficult to make a notional claim that the Pentecostal church is in fact a liberating space for women and gay men, it no longer represents an institutional shackle to be hurriedly discarded in exchange for secular modernity. The church continues to provide a site – although complex and contradictory, in which queer men can express creativity, explore their sexuality, forge solidarity networks, and develop spiritually. It also allows gay men confront the homophobia often present in black communities and allows them to respond to it through performative expression - operating with an awareness of it, rather than denial even though these provisions are available only within a limited framework that dictates to members specific parameters of behaviour.

While Pentecostalism remains socially conservative, within it, it comprises elements that women and gay men can and do utilise to challenge subordination and subvert the status quo. The Pentecostal movement reveals various inherent paradoxes some of which confirm traditional assumptions, but on closer analysis reveal an undercurrent dynamic that is in a state of constant flux.

As the largest collective force in black communities throughout the world, the Pentecostal church is at once reactionary in its embrace of social conservative values yet radical in the genealogy of its infused expression of indigenous African culture with European Christian conventions to produce something entirely new.

Mirroring Nollywood's commercial imperative for global expansion, Nigerian Pentecostals have appropriated a plethora of new media technologies and performative strategies to create a distinctly new artistic language which has revitalised popular culture and transformed the religious landscape not only in Africa, but around the world.

S. PEACE

Illustrations

Fig. 1: Aerial view of the illuminated monument of Christ the Redeemer transformed into a doctor as COVID-19 peaked in Brazil. © Buda Mendes

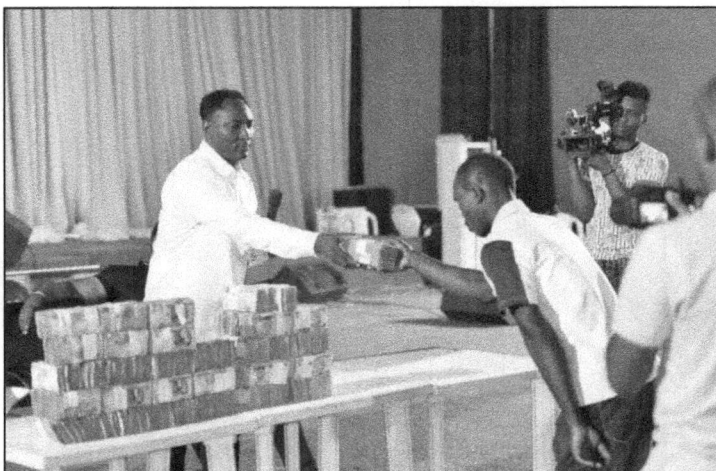

Fig. 2: Prophet Jeremiah Fufeyin of Mercyland Ministry giving out a combined sum of ₦30 million (£60,000) to his followers at a Christmas service in 2018 © Mercyland TV / YouTube

Fig 3: A poster for Rock of Salvation and Liberation Ministries for a Sunday service themed *Operation Vomit my Dollars*. Bonus side attractions promised by Prophet Obidike include 'salvation, release of delayed visas, strange international connections, miracle money, favour from abroad, business boom, and healing.'

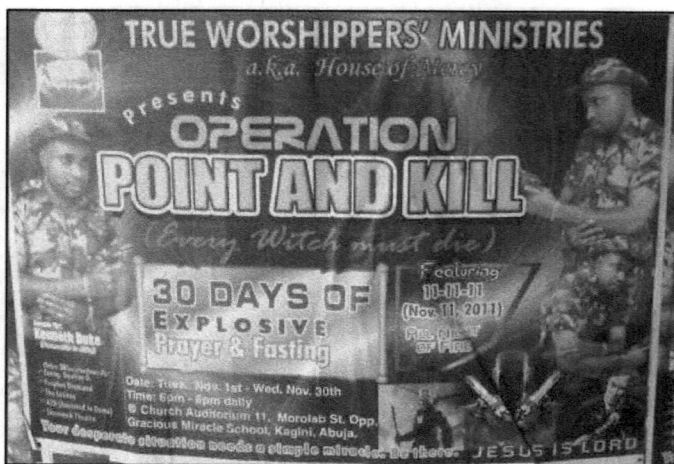

Fig 4: A poster for True Worshippers' Ministries 'House of Mercy' service titled *Operation Point and Kill (Every witch must die)* featuring armed soldiers and imagery from blockbuster action films and video games.

Fig. 5: A 2013 promotional poster for a deliverance service led by 'Lady Apostle' Helen Ukpabio of Liberty Gospel Church featuring a red-eyed wolfdog and a bonfire awaiting witches condemned to burn at the stake.

Fig. 6: A promotional poster for Virgin Glory Intervention Ministries aka the Solution Arena illustrating its Hiroshima Night service with a burning Bible (top left), a lion and a young axe-wielding minister ready to wage combatant and nuclear war against the Devil.

Fig. 7: A 2013 promotional poster for Believers Prophetic Evangelical Chapel
illustrating its weekend of 'prophetic war' with a machete-wielding minister,
themed *Kill them before they kill u*

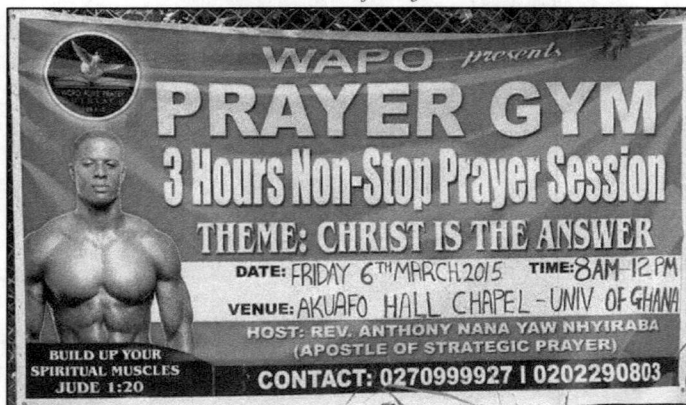

Fig. 8: A 2015 promotional poster for Words Alive Prayer Outreach illustrating a
three-hour non-stop prayer session with a topless bodybuilder urging followers
to "build up your spiritual muscles."

Fig. 9: A Winners' Chapel banner features its leading pastor embedded in an image of a British premier league team popular across Africa, appropriating Chelsea F.C.'s *Home of the Champions* imagery and slogan.

Fig. 10: A woman makes a confession as she is made free of demonic possession during a deliverance service in South Africa.

Fig. 11: A 2018 promotional leaflet by Wordcity Assembly, Enugu
advertising an intimacy workshop aimed at young couples as part of a
Valentine's Day service.

Fig. 12: Members of Zimbabwean-founded Friday Apostles conduct a prayer
session in a woodland near Barnsley estate in South Yorkshire.
© The Friday Apostles

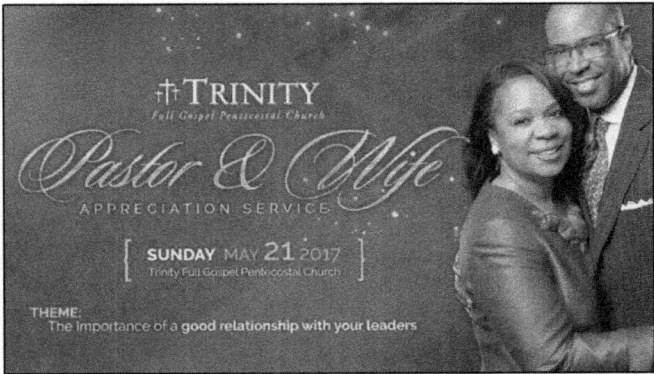

Fig. 13: A 2017 promotional poster for Trinity Full Gospel Pentecostal
Church promoting an appreciation service for both the pastor and his wife.

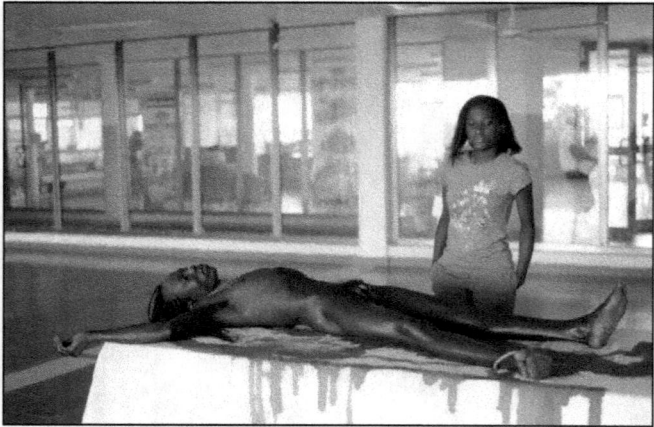

Fig. 14: Ghanaian artist Va-Bene Elikem Fiatsi performing
The First Last Supper in Kumasi, Ghana (2016)
© Va-Bene Elikem Fiatsi / Crazinist Artist

Fig. 15: Nigerian performance artist and political activist Jelili Atiku during a
street performance of *Holy Ovonramwen Cathedral* in Benin City (2014)
© Jelili Atiku

Fig. 16: Kanye West performing with the Sunday Service Choir

Fig. 17: Kanye West and the Sunday Service Choir performing during
Paris Fashion Week at Théâtre des Bouffes du Nord in March 2020
Image © Editorialist

Bibliography

Agina, H. (2010). *The Invasion of the Funky Pastors: Church Business at War with African Culture.*

Anderson, A. (2004). *An introduction to Pentecostalism: Global Charismatic Christianity.* Cambridge: Cambridge University Press.

Apata, G., (2016). *Pentecostalism And Nigeria: New Forms of Religious Life.* PhD. Goldsmiths College, University of London.

Briggs, S. (1987). *Women and Religion* in Drogus, C. A. (1994) *Religious change and women's status in Latin America: a comparison of Catholic base communities and Pentecostal churches.* Notre Dame, Ind.: The Helen Kellogg Institute for International Studies, University of Notre Dame.

Cartier, M. (2013). *Baby, You Are My Religion: Women, Gay Bars, and Theology Before Stonewall* New York: Routledge.

Clarke, P., (1995) *Mahdism In West Africa.* London: Luzac Oriental.

Coleman, M. (2008). *Making a Way out of no Way: A Womanist Theology.* Minneapolis, Minn: Fortress Press.

Cox, H. (2001). *Fire from heaven: The Rise of Pentecostal Spirituality and The Reshaping of Religion in the 21st Century.* Da Capo Press.

Dictionary of African Christian Biography Dacb.org. [online] Available at: <https://dacb.org/>

Dyrness, W., (2001). *Visual Faith: Art, Theology, and Worship in Dialogue.* Baker Publishing Group.

Gbadamosi, T., (1978). *The Growth of Islam Among the Yoruba, 1841-1908*. London: Longman.

Harnischfeger, J., (2006). *State Decline and the Return of Occult Powers: The Case of Prophet Eddy in Nigeria. Magic, Ritual, and Witchcraft*, 1(1), pp.56-78.

Haynes, J., (2016). *Nollywood: The Creation of Nigerian Film Genres*. Chicago, Ill.: University of Chicago Press.

Johnson, E. (2008). *Sweet Tea: Black Gay Men of the South an Oral History*. Chapel Hill: The University of North Carolina Press.

Kalu, O. (2008). *African Pentecostalism*. Oxford: Oxford University Press.

Lewis, G., (1986). *The Look of Magic*. Man, 21(3).

Martin, D. (2002). *Pentecostalism: The World Their Parish*. Oxford [u.a.]: Blackwell.

Nyhagen, L. and Halsaa, B. (2016). *Religion, Gender and Citizenship*. London: Palgrave Macmillan UK.

Oliver, V. et al. (2013). *Radical Presence: Black Performance in Contemporary Art*. Houston: Contemporary Arts Museum.

Ojo, M. (2005). *Religion and Sexuality: Individuality, Choice and Sexual Rights in Nigerian Christianity*. Africa Regional Sexuality Resource Centre

Sanders, G. (2014). *Religious Non-Places: Corporate Megachurches and Their Contributions to Consumer Capitalism*. Critical Sociology.

Wilkinson, M. (2012). *Global Pentecostal Movements. Migration, Mission and Public Religion*. Brill: Leiden, the Netherlands.

Wooldridge, A. and Micklethwait, J. (2014). *God Is Back: How the Global Revival of Faith is Changing the World*. New York: Penguin Books.

Index

ABOUT THE AUTHOR

Sarah Peace is a British-Nigerian writer whose research explores interwoven themes of art, culture, religion and their intersections with gender, rights and freedoms. She is the co-author of *Scott Joplin: One Hundred Years On* (2017) and the editor of *WordPower: Language as Medium* (2019). She holds an M.A. in Art and Politics from Goldsmiths, University of London. She lives in the UK where she also produces work as a visual artist under a pseudonym.

www.ingramcontent.com/pod-product-compliance
Lightning Source LLC
Chambersburg PA
CBHW070805050426
42452CB00011B/1908